While every precaution has been taken in the preparation of this book, the publisher assumes no responsibility for errors or omissions, or for damages resulting from the use of the information contained herein.

MINDFUL PARENTING: RAISING EMOTIONALLY INTELLIGENT CHILDREN

First edition. April 26, 2024.

ISBN: 979-8224150564

Written by Neo K. Bika.

Table of Contents

Mindful Parenting: Raising Emotionally Intelligent Children

Neo K. Bika

Preface

Welcome to "Mindful Parenting: Raising Emotionally Intelligent Children." As you embark on this journey with us, we invite you to explore the profound impact of mindful parenting on your child's emotional well-being and overall development.

In today's fast-paced world, the demands and challenges of parenting can often feel overwhelming. Amidst the hustle and bustle of daily life, it's easy to lose sight of the importance of cultivating emotional intelligence in our children. However, research has shown time and again that emotional intelligence plays a crucial role in determining a child's success, happiness, and resilience in life.

As a children's ministry teacher with years of experience working with families, I've witnessed firsthand the transformative power of mindful parenting. This book is a culmination of my insights, experiences, and the latest research in child development psychology and mindfulness practices.

In the pages that follow, we'll delve deep into the heart of mindful parenting, exploring its fundamental principles, practical strategies, and real-life applications. From cultivating self-awareness and emotional intelligence to fostering a nurturing family environment and navigating parenting challenges, each chapter is designed to provide you with valuable insights and actionable steps to become a more mindful and effective parent.

But mindful parenting isn't just about techniques and strategies; it's about fostering a deeper connection with your child and nurturing their inner world. It's about creating a safe and supportive environment where they feel seen, heard, and valued. It's about guiding them on their journey of self-discovery and growth, empowering them to navigate life's ups and downs with resilience and grace.

Throughout this book, you'll find practical exercises, reflection thoughts, and real-life insights to guide you on your mindful parenting journey. Whether you're a new parent navigating the early years of infancy or a seasoned parent facing the challenges of adolescence, there's something here for everyone.

As you read through these pages, I encourage you to approach the material with an open heart and mind. Embrace the principles of mindfulness and compassion not only in your parenting but also in your own self-care journey. Remember that mindful parenting is a practice, not a destination, and that every moment is an opportunity to deepen your connection with your child and cultivate their emotional intelligence.

I'm thrilled to accompany you on this journey of mindful parenting, and I'm confident that together, we can create a more harmonious and fulfilling family life. So let's dive in, with curiosity, compassion, and a willingness to embrace the transformative power of mindful parenting.

Part 1: The Power of Mindful Parenting

Introduction to Mindful Parenting

Welcome to the journey of mindful parenting! In the whirlwind of raising a child, it's easy to feel swept away by daily tasks and emotional demands. This book offers a path to reconnect with yourself and your child, fostering a deeper understanding and a more fulfilling experience for both of you.

Mindful parenting is the practice of bringing awareness and intentionality to your interactions with your child. It's about being present in the moment, with all its challenges and joys. By cultivating skills like focused attention, non-judgmental acceptance, and emotional regulation, you can navigate the ups and downs of parenthood with greater calmness and compassion.

This book is your guide to embracing mindfulness in your parenting journey. We'll explore the core principles of mindful parenting, unveil its benefits for you and your child, and provide practical exercises you can integrate into your daily life. Whether you're a new parent or a seasoned pro, mindful parenting offers valuable tools to strengthen your connection, manage stress, and nurture a more peaceful and joyful family environment.

Are you ready to embark on this transformative journey? Let's begin!

Overview of the Book's Content and Goals

In the chapters that follow, we'll dive deeper into the principles and practices of mindful parenting, exploring topics such as cultivating self-awareness, building emotional intelligence in children, fostering a growth mindset and emotional resilience, and navigating the challenges of parenting with mindfulness and compassion.

As we embark on this journey together, I invite you to approach it with an open heart and an open mind. Embrace the journey of self-discovery and growth that mindful parenting offers, and trust in the transformative power of presence, intention, and love. Together, we can create a more harmonious and fulfilling family life, grounded in the principles of mindfulness and compassion.

Defining mindful parenting entails delving into its multifaceted nature, encompassing awareness, presence, and intentionality in the parental role. At its core, mindful parenting is an approach that encourages parents to cultivate a deep sense of consciousness and attentiveness in their interactions with their children. It involves being fully present in the moment, both mentally and emotionally, with an unwavering focus on the needs and experiences of the child.

Awareness forms the cornerstone of mindful parenting, urging parents to tune into their own thoughts, emotions, and reactions, as well as those of their children. It involves developing a keen sense of self-awareness, allowing parents to recognize and understand their own triggers, biases, and patterns of behavior. Through this heightened awareness, parents can respond to their children with greater empathy, patience, and understanding, fostering a more harmonious parent-child dynamic.

Presence is another fundamental aspect of mindful parenting, emphasizing the importance of being fully engaged and available to our children at each moment. It entails setting aside distractions, such as smartphones or work-related concerns, and immersing ourselves wholeheartedly in the present experience with our children. By cultivating a state of presence, parents can forge deeper connections with their children, nurturing feelings of security, trust, and belonging.

Intentionality rounds out the triad of mindful parenting, urging parents to approach their role with purpose, clarity, and conscious decision-making. It involves setting clear intentions and goals for our parenting journey, grounded in our values, beliefs, and aspirations for our children. Intentional parenting invites us to make deliberate choices in how we respond to our children, ensuring that our actions align with our overarching vision for their well-being and development.

In essence, mindful parenting is a holistic approach that empowers parents to cultivate a nurturing and supportive environment for their children. It encourages us to embody qualities of awareness, presence, and intentionality in our parenting practices, fostering deeper connections, stronger bonds, and greater emotional resilience within the family unit. By embracing the principles of mindful parenting, parents can embark on a transformative journey of growth, self-discovery, and mutual understanding with their children.

Chapter 1: Understanding Mindful Parenting

Mindful Parenting Definitions

1. Scientific Definition:

Mindful parenting can be defined as an approach rooted in the principles of mindfulness meditation, adapted to the context of parenting. It involves cultivating non-judgmental awareness, present-moment attention, and compassionate acceptance in one's interactions with their children. Scientific research supports the benefits of mindful parenting in promoting children's emotional regulation, resilience, and overall well-being, as well as enhancing parent-child relationships.

2. Psychological Definition:

From a psychological perspective, mindful parenting is characterized by a parent's ability to respond to their child with empathy, acceptance, and emotional attunement. It involves being fully present and engaged in the parent-child interaction, fostering a secure attachment and promoting the child's socio-emotional development. Mindful parenting practices draw upon principles of attachment theory, cognitive-behavioral therapy, and interpersonal neurobiology to nurture healthy parent-child relationships.

3. Developmental Definition:

In terms of child development, mindful parenting can be defined as an approach that recognizes and responds to the unique needs and developmental stages of children. It involves adapting parenting strategies and communication styles to support children's evolving cognitive, emotional, and social skills. Mindful parenting encourages parents to scaffold their children's learning experiences, provide age-appropriate guidance, and foster autonomy within a supportive and nurturing environment.

4. Theological Definition:

From a theological perspective, mindful parenting reflects a commitment to embodying spiritual virtues such as presence, compassion, and unconditional love in one's parenting practices. It involves recognizing the sacredness and inherent dignity of each child as a divine gift entrusted to their care. Mindful parenting aligns with religious teachings on stewardship, responsibility, and the importance of nurturing the spiritual and moral development of children within the family unit.

5. Holistic Definition:

Finally, a holistic definition of mindful parenting integrates elements from various disciplines, encompassing physical, emotional, cognitive, and spiritual dimensions of parenting. It emphasizes the interconnectedness of mind, body, and spirit in the parent-child relationship and advocates for a balanced and integrated approach to child-rearing. Mindful parenting encourages parents to cultivate self-awareness, resilience, and authenticity, fostering a sense of wholeness and well-being for both parent and child.

But Seriously What the Heck is Mindful Parenting?

What is mindful parenting, you may ask? At its core, mindful parenting is about bringing a sense of awareness, presence, and intentionality to the parenting journey. It's about cultivating a deeper understanding of ourselves as parents, as well as our children, and nurturing a strong, supportive connection that fosters emotional growth and well-being.

In today's fast-paced world, where distractions abound and pressures are ever-present, mindful parenting offers a sanctuary of calm amidst the chaos. It invites us to slow down, to pause, and to be fully present with our children in each moment. It's about tuning in to their needs, their emotions, and their unique perspectives, and responding with empathy, compassion, and understanding.

But mindful parenting is not just about being present in the moment; it's also about being intentional in our actions and our interactions with our children. It's about making conscious choices that are guided by our values, our beliefs, and our vision for the kind of parents we want to be and the kind of relationships we want to cultivate with our children.

As we embark on this journey of mindful parenting together, it's important to recognize the importance of emotional intelligence in children. Emotional intelligence, or EQ, encompasses a range of skills, including self-awareness, self-regulation, empathy, and social skills, that are crucial for navigating life's challenges, building healthy relationships, and achieving success and fulfillment in life.

By embracing mindful parenting practices, we have the opportunity to nurture these essential EQ skills in our children and lay the foundation for their future happiness and success. But mindful parenting is not just about the benefits it brings to our children; it's also about the profound impact it has on us as parents.

Through the practice of mindful parenting, we have the opportunity to deepen our own self-awareness, to cultivate greater empathy and compassion for ourselves and others, and to experience more joy, fulfillment, and peace in our roles as parents. It's a journey of personal growth and transformation that extends far beyond the parent-child relationship and touches every aspect of our lives.

Core Components of Emotional Intelligence

Emotional Intelligence (EI), also known as emotional quotient (EQ), is a complex set of skills that goes beyond simply being "good" with emotions. It's about understanding your own emotional landscape, managing those emotions effectively, and using that knowledge to navigate your interactions with the world around you. Here's a deeper dive into the five core components of EI:

1. Self-Awareness: This is the bedrock of EI. It's the ability to recognize your emotions as they arise, and to understand how they're influencing your thoughts and behaviors. Imagine you're giving a presentation and your heart starts racing. Self-awareness allows you to identify this as nervousness, not excitement, and choose a calming strategy like deep breathing. Self-aware individuals can also identify their emotional strengths and weaknesses. For example, someone who is aware they tend to get frustrated easily can take steps to manage that tendency before it derails a situation.

2. Self-Regulation: Once you've identified your emotions, self-regulation allows you to manage them in a healthy way. This involves the ability to delay gratification, control impulses, and channel your emotions constructively. Instead of letting anger lead to a heated argument, self-regulation allows you to take a step back, calm yourself down, and communicate your needs assertively. People with strong self-regulation are less likely to be ruled by their emotions and can make more deliberate choices.

3. Social Awareness: This component is all about picking up on the emotions of others. It involves being attuned to nonverbal cues like body language and facial expressions, and understanding the emotional undercurrents of a situation. Imagine a colleague seems withdrawn during a meeting. Social awareness allows you to recognize they might be feeling down and approach them with empathy, offering support or simply listening.

4. Relationship Skills: This component involves using your emotional intelligence to build and maintain strong relationships. It encompasses effective communication skills, active listening, conflict resolution, and the ability to build trust and rapport. People with strong relationship skills can navigate social interactions smoothly, fostering positive connections and resolving disagreements constructively. Imagine you have a disagreement with a friend. Relationship skills allow you to express your feelings clearly while also considering your friend's perspective, working towards a solution that works for both of you.

5. Motivation: This refers to your internal drive to achieve your goals and pursue what matters to you. It involves setting goals, staying focused, and persevering through challenges. Emotionally intelligent individuals are intrinsically motivated, finding ways to stay inspired even when faced with setbacks. Think about a student who struggles with a particular subject but doesn't give up. Motivation allows them to seek help, develop strategies, and keep pushing towards their academic goals.

By developing these core components, individuals can increase their emotional intelligence and navigate life's challenges more effectively. It's a journey of self-discovery and continuous learning, but the rewards of stronger relationships, greater self-control, and a more fulfilling life make it a worthwhile pursuit.

Importance of Emotional Intelligence in Children

1. Foundation for Social and Emotional Well-being:

The foundation for social and emotional well-being in children lies in the development of emotional intelligence, which serves as the cornerstone of their psychological health and resilience. Emotional intelligence encompasses a set of skills and abilities that enable children to recognize, understand, and manage their own emotions, as well as navigate interpersonal relationships effectively.

At its core, emotional intelligence equips children with the tools to identify and label their emotions accurately. By gaining insight into their feelings, children can better understand the underlying reasons for their emotional experiences and respond to them in constructive ways. This self-awareness forms the basis for emotional regulation, allowing children to manage their emotions in adaptive ways and avoid being overwhelmed by intense or distressing feelings.

Moreover, emotional intelligence enables children to empathize with others and understand their perspectives and emotions. Empathy is a fundamental aspect of social interaction, fostering compassion, cooperation, and kindness towards others. By recognizing and validating the emotions of their peers, children can build stronger interpersonal connections and foster a sense of belonging within their social groups.

Additionally, emotional intelligence enhances children's ability to communicate effectively and resolve conflicts peacefully. By expressing their emotions assertively and listening empathetically to others, children can navigate interpersonal challenges with confidence and diplomacy. These communication skills are essential for building positive relationships and fostering a supportive social environment.

Furthermore, emotional intelligence plays a crucial role in children's overall mental health and resilience. Children who possess higher levels of emotional intelligence are better equipped to cope with stress, adversity, and setbacks. They can draw upon a repertoire of coping strategies to manage challenging situations and bounce back from setbacks with resilience and optimism.

2. Academic Success and Learning Readiness:

Academic success and learning readiness are deeply intertwined with emotional intelligence in children, as they play a pivotal role in shaping cognitive development, academic performance, and overall learning outcomes. By fostering emotional intelligence, children are better prepared to engage in learning activities, navigate academic challenges, and excel in educational settings.

One aspect of emotional intelligence that contributes to academic success is self-regulation. Children who possess strong self-regulation skills are better able to manage their attention, impulses, and behaviors in the classroom, allowing them to stay focused and on task during learning activities. By regulating their emotions effectively, children can minimize distractions and maintain optimal levels of arousal, which is essential for efficient information processing and learning retention.

Moreover, emotional intelligence enhances children's ability to cope with academic stress and setbacks. By developing resilience and coping mechanisms, children can navigate academic challenges with confidence and perseverance. Instead of becoming overwhelmed by failure or criticism, emotionally intelligent children are more likely to view setbacks as learning opportunities and persist in their efforts to achieve academic goals.

Furthermore, emotional intelligence fosters positive relationships with teachers and peers, which are essential for creating a supportive learning environment. Children who are emotionally intelligent are better equipped to communicate effectively, resolve conflicts peacefully, and collaborate with others, facilitating cooperative learning and peer support.

Additionally, emotionally intelligent children are more empathetic and understanding of their classmates' perspectives and experiences, which contributes to a sense of inclusivity and belonging in the classroom. Emotional intelligence also plays a crucial role in enhancing children's critical thinking and problem-solving skills.

By developing the ability to recognize and understand their own emotions, children can better regulate their thought processes and make informed decisions. Moreover, empathy and perspective-taking enable children to consider multiple viewpoints and approaches when faced with academic challenges, leading to more creative and innovative problem-solving strategies.

3. Conflict Resolution and Peer Relationships:

Conflict resolution and peer relationships are vital aspects of a child's social and emotional development, and emotional intelligence plays a significant role in shaping these areas. By fostering emotional intelligence, children can navigate conflicts effectively, build positive relationships with their peers, and cultivate a supportive social network.

One key component of emotional intelligence relevant to conflict resolution is self-awareness. Children who are emotionally intelligent possess a keen understanding of their own emotions, including how they feel and why they feel that way. This self-awareness enables them to recognize when conflicts arise and understand their own role in contributing to or exacerbating the situation. By acknowledging their emotions and their impact on their behavior, children can take proactive steps to manage their responses and engage in constructive conflict resolution strategies.

Moreover, emotional intelligence facilitates empathy and perspective-taking, which are essential for understanding the thoughts, feelings, and perspectives of others involved in a conflict. Empathetic children are better able to put themselves in someone else's shoes, see things from their point of view, and recognize the underlying needs and motivations driving their behavior. This empathy fosters compassion, understanding, and cooperation, laying the foundation for effective communication and conflict resolution.

Furthermore, emotionally intelligent children possess strong interpersonal skills, such as active listening, communication, and negotiation, which are essential for resolving conflicts and building positive peer relationships. By actively listening to others, children can validate their feelings, clarify misunderstandings, and find common ground for compromise. Effective communication enables children to express themselves clearly, assert their needs and boundaries, and engage in collaborative problem-solving with their peers.

In addition, emotional intelligence promotes emotional regulation, which is crucial for managing intense emotions and de-escalating conflicts. Children who are emotionally intelligent can recognize when their emotions are escalating and employ strategies to calm themselves down, such as deep breathing, mindfulness techniques, or taking a break from the situation. By staying calm and composed during conflicts, children can approach resolution with clarity, patience, and empathy, fostering positive outcomes and maintaining positive relationships with their peers.

Moreover, emotional intelligence fosters resilience and adaptability, which are essential for bouncing back from conflicts and maintaining healthy peer relationships over time. Resilient children are better able to cope with setbacks, learn from their experiences, and bounce back stronger than before. By viewing conflicts as opportunities for growth and learning, emotionally intelligent children can navigate challenges with confidence and resilience, strengthening their interpersonal skills and building stronger, more resilient peer relationships in the process.

4. Self-awareness and Identity Development

Self-awareness and identity development are fundamental aspects of emotional intelligence in children, playing a pivotal role in their overall social and emotional well-being. By fostering self-awareness, parents and caregivers can help children develop a deeper understanding of themselves, their emotions, and their unique identity, laying the foundation for healthy self-esteem, confidence, and resilience.

Self-awareness encompasses the ability to recognize and understand one's own thoughts, feelings, strengths, weaknesses, and values. Children who are self-aware have a clear understanding of their emotions, including how they feel and why they feel that way. This awareness enables them to accurately identify and label their emotions, differentiate between different feelings, and understand the underlying reasons behind their emotional responses. By developing this level of self-awareness, children can gain insight into their own needs, preferences, and desires, empowering them to make informed choices and navigate life's challenges more effectively.

Moreover, self-awareness is closely linked to identity development, as children begin to form a sense of self and establish their own identity based on their experiences, relationships, and personal characteristics. Through self-reflection and introspection, children explore their interests, values, beliefs, and goals, shaping their identity and sense of self over time. By encouraging children to explore their own identities and express themselves authentically, parents and caregivers can support their journey of self-discovery and help them develop a strong, positive sense of self.

Furthermore, self-awareness plays a crucial role in fostering empathy and understanding towards others. Children who are self-aware are better able to recognize and empathize with the thoughts, feelings, and perspectives of others, as they have a deeper understanding of their own emotions and experiences. This empathy promotes compassion, kindness, and cooperation, enhancing children's interpersonal relationships and contributing to a more inclusive and empathetic society.

Additionally, self-awareness facilitates emotional regulation, which is essential for managing stress, anxiety, and other intense emotions. Children who are self-aware can identify when their emotions are escalating and employ strategies to calm themselves down, such as deep breathing, positive self-talk, or seeking support from trusted adults. By developing this ability to regulate their emotions, children can cope more effectively with life's challenges, maintain a sense of balance and stability, and make healthy decisions based on their own needs and values.

5. Behavioral Regulation and Coping Skills:

Behavioral regulation and coping skills are essential components of emotional intelligence in children, playing a crucial role in their ability to manage stress, regulate their emotions, and engage in adaptive behaviors. By developing these skills, children can effectively navigate challenging situations, cope with adversity, and make healthy choices that promote their overall well-being.

One key aspect of behavioral regulation is the ability to modulate one's behavior in response to different situations and demands. Children who possess strong behavioral regulation skills can regulate their impulses, control their emotions, and exhibit appropriate conduct in various contexts. This skill enables them to adapt to changing circumstances, follow rules and instructions, and interact positively with others, fostering positive relationships and social competence.

Moreover, behavioral regulation encompasses the ability to delay gratification and resist impulsive behaviors, which is critical for achieving long-term goals and success. Children who can delay gratification are better able to plan, set goals, and persist in the face of obstacles, enhancing their academic achievement, personal growth, and overall life outcomes. By teaching children strategies for impulse control and self-discipline, parents and caregivers can empower them to make thoughtful decisions, resist peer pressure, and act in accordance with their values and goals.

Additionally, coping skills are essential for helping children manage stress, adversity, and negative emotions effectively. Coping skills encompass a range of strategies and techniques that children can use to regulate their emotions, reduce stress, and cope with challenging situations. These may include problem-solving skills, emotion regulation techniques, relaxation exercises, and seeking support from others. By teaching children adaptive coping skills, parents and caregivers can equip them with the tools they need to navigate life's ups and downs, build resilience, and maintain emotional well-being.

Furthermore, developing behavioral regulation and coping skills can have far-reaching benefits for children's mental health and academic success. Research has shown that children who possess strong coping skills are better able to cope with stress, anxiety, and depression, reducing their risk of developing mental health problems later in life. Additionally, children who exhibit strong behavioral regulation skills are more likely to excel academically, as they can focus their attention, manage their time effectively, and engage in productive learning behaviors.

6. Empathy and Compassion:

Empathy and compassion are fundamental aspects of emotional intelligence in children, shaping their ability to understand and respond to the emotions and experiences of others. When children develop empathy, they demonstrate an awareness of the feelings, needs, and perspectives of those around them, fostering deeper connections and more meaningful relationships. Compassion, on the other hand, involves not only understanding others' emotions but also feeling a genuine concern for their well-being and a desire to alleviate their suffering.

One of the key benefits of nurturing empathy and compassion in children is the promotion of positive interpersonal relationships. When children are empathetic, they are better able to communicate effectively, resolve conflicts peacefully, and build trust and rapport with their peers and family members. By understanding others' perspectives and emotions, children can navigate social interactions with sensitivity and kindness, fostering a sense of belonging and acceptance within their communities.

Furthermore, empathy and compassion play a vital role in promoting prosocial behaviors and altruism in children. When children empathize with others' feelings and experiences, they are more likely to engage in acts of kindness, generosity, and cooperation, contributing to a more compassionate and caring society. By encouraging children to consider the needs of others and respond with compassion, parents and caregivers can instill values of empathy, altruism, and social responsibility, shaping them into empathetic and compassionate individuals who contribute positively to their communities.

Moreover, empathy and compassion are essential for fostering a sense of global citizenship and promoting social justice and equity. When children develop empathy for individuals from diverse backgrounds and cultures, they are better equipped to challenge stereotypes, prejudice, and discrimination, promoting inclusivity and understanding in their communities. By nurturing empathy and compassion, parents and caregivers can empower children to become agents of positive change, advocating for justice, equality, and compassion for all.

Additionally, cultivating empathy and compassion in children has significant benefits for their own emotional well-being and mental health. Research has shown that children who demonstrate empathy and compassion are more resilient to stress, anxiety, and depression, as they have strong social support networks and coping mechanisms. By fostering empathy and compassion, parents and caregivers can promote children's emotional resilience, helping them navigate life's challenges with grace, empathy, and compassion.

7. Long-term Success and Well-being:

The development of emotional intelligence in children is not only crucial for their immediate social and emotional well-being but also has long-term implications for their success and overall well-being throughout life. When children possess strong emotional intelligence skills, they are better equipped to navigate the complexities of adulthood and face the challenges that arise in various domains of life.

One aspect of long-term success linked to emotional intelligence is academic achievement. Research has consistently shown that children with higher levels of emotional intelligence tend to perform better academically, exhibiting greater focus, motivation, and resilience in their studies. By understanding their emotions and managing stress effectively, these children can concentrate more effectively on their studies, engage in effective problem-solving, and persevere through academic challenges with greater resilience.

Moreover, emotional intelligence plays a significant role in shaping children's future career success and professional relationships. In today's rapidly changing and interconnected world, employers increasingly value employees who possess strong interpersonal skills, such as empathy, communication, and conflict resolution. Individuals with high emotional intelligence are better able to collaborate effectively with colleagues, communicate clearly and persuasively, and adapt to changing work environments, making them valuable assets in the workplace.

Furthermore, emotional intelligence contributes to overall mental health and well-being, reducing the likelihood of developing mental health disorders such as anxiety, depression, and substance abuse later in life. Children who learn to recognize and regulate their emotions effectively are less likely to experience chronic stress and burnout, leading to better mental and emotional health outcomes in adulthood.

In addition to academic and career success, emotional intelligence is also linked to success in relationships and personal life. Individuals who possess strong emotional intelligence skills are better equipped to form and maintain healthy, fulfilling relationships, as they are more adept at communicating their needs, understanding the perspectives of others, and resolving conflicts constructively. By cultivating empathy, compassion, and effective communication skills from an early age, children develop the foundation for healthy and meaningful relationships throughout their lives.

Moreover, emotional intelligence contributes to overall life satisfaction and happiness, as individuals who are emotionally intelligent tend to have a greater sense of self-awareness, purpose, and resilience in the face of life's challenges. By learning to navigate their emotions effectively, children develop the skills to cope with adversity, bounce back from setbacks, and find meaning and fulfillment in their lives.

Chapter 2: The Mindful Parent: Your Journey Begins

Benefits of Mindful Parenting for Parents

1. Reduced Stress

One of the most profound benefits of mindful parenting is its ability to significantly reduce stress levels in parents. Parenting can be an incredibly rewarding experience, but it also brings with it numerous challenges, demands, and pressures that can contribute to chronic stress and burnout. Mindful parenting provides a powerful antidote to this stress by encouraging parents to stay anchored in the present moment, letting go of worries about the past or future.

When parents are fully present and engaged with their children, they are better able to respond to their needs with clarity, patience, and emotional regulation. This present-moment awareness prevents parents from becoming overwhelmed by the constant stream of thoughts, worries, and external pressures that can fuel stress and anxiety. Instead of getting caught up in ruminating over past mistakes or agonizing over future concerns, mindful parents can channel their full attention and energy into the here and now, allowing them to respond to their child's needs calmly and effectively.

Mindfulness practices, such as meditation and deep breathing exercises, also play a crucial role in reducing stress levels. These practices help parents cultivate a sense of inner calm and emotional balance, enabling them to navigate the ups and downs of parenting with greater equanimity. By learning to observe their thoughts and emotions with a non-judgmental attitude, parents can disengage from negative thought patterns and unhelpful emotional reactions that can exacerbate stress.

Additionally, mindful parenting encourages parents to let go of unrealistic expectations and self-criticism. Perfectionism and harsh self-judgment can be major sources of stress for parents who constantly berate themselves for perceived failures or shortcomings. Mindfulness teaches parents to embrace self-compassion and acknowledge that imperfection is an inherent part of the human experience. This shift in perspective can alleviate the self-imposed pressure and stress that often accompanies parenting.

Reduced stress levels have far-reaching benefits for both parents and children. When parents are less stressed, they are better able to provide a nurturing and emotionally supportive environment for their children. They are more patient, more present, and better equipped to handle the inevitable challenges of parenting with grace and composure. This, in turn, can foster a sense of security and emotional well-being in children, contributing to their overall healthy development.

2. Greater Patience

Patience is a virtue that is essential for effective parenting, yet it can often be elusive in the face of the daily demands and frustrations that come with raising children. Mindful parenting offers a powerful pathway to cultivating greater patience, enabling parents to respond to their child's behavior with thoughtfulness, empathy, and composure.

At the core of mindful parenting is the practice of pausing before reacting. In the heat of a challenging moment, when a child's behavior triggers an impulsive emotional response, mindful parents learn to take a conscious breath and create a space between the stimulus and their reaction. This simple act of pausing disrupts the automatic, knee-jerk reactions that can lead to harsh words or actions that parents may later regret.

During this pause, mindful parents can bring their attention to the present moment, observing their own emotional state and the situation at hand with a non-judgmental awareness. This present-moment awareness allows them to respond from a place of clarity and intentionality, rather than being driven by reactive impulses or habitual patterns of behavior.

Moreover, mindfulness cultivates a deeper sense of empathy and compassion, which are essential for patience. By practicing non-judgmental acceptance of their child's thoughts, feelings, and behaviors, mindful parents develop a greater understanding of the underlying needs or emotions that may be driving their child's actions. This empathetic perspective enables them to respond with kindness and patience, rather than frustration or harsh discipline.

Mindfulness also fosters emotional regulation, a key component of patience. Through practices such as meditation and deep breathing exercises, parents learn to manage their own emotional reactions more effectively. When faced with a challenging situation, they can consciously choose to respond with a calm, centered presence, rather than being swept away by intense emotions like anger or frustration.

Mindful parenting encourages parents to let go of unrealistic expectations and perfectionism, which can be significant contributors to impatience. By embracing a non-judgmental attitude towards themselves and their children, parents can cultivate acceptance and patience for the imperfections and challenges that are inherent in the parenting journey.

Greater patience not only benefits parents by reducing stress and promoting more positive interactions with their children, but it also has a profound impact on children's development. When children experience patience and understanding from their parents, they feel more secure, valued, and respected. This sense of emotional safety creates an environment conducive to healthy emotional and social development, fostering resilience, self-regulation, and positive relationships.

3. Improved Emotional Regulation

Emotional regulation is a critical skill for parents, as it enables them to navigate the often turbulent waters of parenting with grace, composure, and intentionality. Mindful parenting provides a powerful framework for cultivating this essential ability by helping parents become more aware of their own emotions and triggers, and equipping them with tools to effectively manage and respond to their feelings.

At the heart of mindful parenting is the practice of present-moment awareness. Through techniques such as meditation and mindful breathing, parents learn to tune into their internal experiences, including their thoughts, emotions, and physical sensations. This heightened awareness allows them to recognize emotional patterns and triggers as they arise, rather than being blindsided by intense feelings or reacting impulsively.

When parents are able to recognize their emotions with clarity, they can then employ various mindfulness-based strategies to regulate and respond to those emotions in a healthy manner. For example, mindful breathing exercises can help parents diffuse intense emotions like anger or frustration, preventing outbursts or conflicts that may arise from unresolved feelings. Practicing self-compassion and non-judgmental acceptance can also help parents let go of negative emotions more easily, rather than getting caught in cycles of rumination or self-criticism.

Moreover, mindful parenting encourages parents to cultivate a "pause" between the arising of an emotion and their response to it. This pause, however brief, creates a space for parents to observe their emotions without immediately acting on them. Within this pause, parents can consciously choose how to respond in a way that aligns with their values and the well-being of their children, rather than being driven by reactive impulses.

Improved emotional regulation also has ripple effects on the parent-child relationship and the overall family dynamic. When parents are able to regulate their emotions effectively, they create a calmer, more stable emotional environment for their children. This sense of emotional safety and consistency can foster a deeper connection between parents and children, as well as promote healthy emotional development in children themselves.

Furthermore, parents who are skilled at emotional regulation can model these valuable skills for their children. By observing their parents' ability to manage intense emotions with mindfulness and self-control, children learn important lessons about emotional intelligence and self-regulation, which can serve them well throughout their lives.

4. Enhanced Parent-Child Communication

Effective communication is the bedrock of strong, healthy parent-child relationships. However, in the busyness and distractions of modern life, meaningful communication can often take a backseat. Mindful parenting places a strong emphasis on cultivating active listening and empathetic communication skills, enabling parents to build deeper connections and understanding with their children.

At the core of mindful communication is the practice of presence and attunement. When parents approach interactions with their children with a mindful, non-judgmental awareness, they are better able to tune into their child's verbal and non-verbal cues, truly listening to what is being said, as well as what is not being said. This level of attunement allows parents to pick up on their child's underlying emotions, needs, and perspectives, fostering a sense of being heard and understood.

Mindful parents also employ the skill of active listening, which involves giving their full attention to their child without interrupting or formulating responses while the child is speaking. By setting aside distractions and fully engaging in the present moment, parents create a space for their child to express themselves freely, without feeling rushed or dismissed.

Empathetic communication is another hallmark of mindful parenting. Through practices like mindful listening and non-judgmental observation, parents develop the ability to see situations from their child's perspective, acknowledging and validating their child's thoughts and feelings without minimizing or dismissing them. This empathetic approach builds trust and emotional safety, encouraging children to open up and share their innermost experiences with their parents.

Additionally, mindful parenting emphasizes the importance of clear, compassionate communication from parents. By cultivating emotional awareness and regulation, parents can express themselves in a calm, thoughtful manner, even during challenging or emotionally charged situations. This mindful approach to communication helps prevent defensive reactions or escalations of conflict, promoting understanding and collaboration between parents and children.

Enhanced parent-child communication has far-reaching benefits for the entire family. When children feel heard, understood, and accepted by their parents, they are more likely to develop strong self-esteem, emotional resilience, and positive relationships with others. Open and empathetic communication also fosters a sense of emotional safety and trust within the family, creating an environment where children feel comfortable expressing their needs, concerns, and vulnerabilities.

5. Improved Problem-Solving Skills

Parenting is rife with challenges, conflicts, and issues that require creative problem-solving skills. From navigating sibling rivalries to addressing behavioral issues or academic struggles, parents are constantly called upon to find effective solutions. Mindful parenting provides a powerful framework for enhancing problem-solving abilities by cultivating a calm, clear, and non-judgmental mindset.

One of the key principles of mindful parenting is present-moment awareness. By anchoring their attention in the here and now, parents can approach problems with a heightened sense of clarity and objectivity. Rather than being clouded by rumination over past events or anxieties about the future, mindful parents can observe the problem at hand with a fresh perspective, free from preconceptions or reactive impulses.

This present-moment awareness also allows parents to tune into their own thought processes and emotional states, enabling them to recognize when they may be approaching a problem from a place of bias, stress, or reactivity. Mindfulness practices, such as deep breathing or meditation, can help parents regulate their emotions and cultivate a sense of calm, which is essential for effective problem-solving.

Furthermore, mindful parenting encourages parents to approach challenges with a non-judgmental and curious attitude. Rather than immediately jumping to conclusions or assigning blame, mindful parents can step back and observe the situation from multiple angles, considering diverse perspectives and potential contributing factors. This open-minded approach often leads to more creative and innovative solutions.

Mindfulness also fosters cognitive flexibility, a key component of problem-solving. By practicing non-attachment to fixed ideas or preconceived notions, parents can more readily consider alternative viewpoints and potential solutions. This cognitive flexibility allows them to adapt and pivot their approach as needed, rather than stubbornly clinging to strategies that may not be effective.

Moreover, mindful parenting emphasizes the importance of collaboration and open communication in problem-solving. By creating a safe and non-judgmental space for dialogue, parents can involve their children in the problem-solving process, soliciting their input and perspectives. This collaborative approach not only leads to more inclusive and effective solutions but also teaches children valuable problem-solving skills that they can carry into adulthood.

Improved problem-solving skills have far-reaching benefits for the entire family dynamic. When parents can approach challenges with a calm, clear, and creative mindset, they are better equipped to find lasting solutions that address the root causes of issues, rather than merely treating symptoms. This proactive approach can prevent conflicts from escalating and can foster a more harmonious and resilient family environment.

In essence, mindful parenting cultivates the essential qualities of present-moment awareness, emotional regulation, cognitive flexibility, and open-mindedness – all of which contribute to enhanced problem-solving abilities. By embracing these principles, parents can navigate the inevitable challenges of parenting with greater wisdom, creativity, and effectiveness.

6. Modeling Healthy Behavior

Children learn a significant portion of their behaviors, values, and life skills through observing and imitating their parents. As such, parents have a profound opportunity – and responsibility – to serve as positive role models, demonstrating the attitudes and practices they wish to instill in their children. Mindful parenting provides a framework for embodying and modeling healthy behaviors that can have a lasting impact on a child's development.

One of the core aspects of mindful parenting is emotional self-awareness and regulation. By practicing mindfulness techniques such as meditation, deep breathing, and present-moment awareness, parents can learn to recognize and manage their own emotions in a healthy manner. When children witness their parents navigating intense feelings with composure, mindfulness, and self-control, they are provided with a powerful example of how to regulate their own emotional experiences.

Effective communication is another area where mindful parents can lead by example. Through practices like active listening, empathetic responding, and clear, compassionate expression, parents model the skills necessary for building strong, positive relationships. Children who observe their parents communicating mindfully are more likely to develop these valuable interpersonal abilities themselves.

Mindful parenting also emphasizes the cultivation of compassion, both towards oneself and towards others. When parents approach themselves and their children with a non-judgmental, accepting attitude, they demonstrate the power of self-compassion and kindness. This modeling can help children develop a healthier self-concept and a greater capacity for empathy and understanding towards others.

Mindful parents often prioritize self-care and work-life balance, recognizing the importance of tending to their own physical, emotional, and spiritual needs. By carving out time for personal growth, relaxation, and rejuvenation, parents show their children the value of self-nurturing and prevent burnout or resentment from impacting their parenting.

Importantly, mindful parenting does not require perfection; rather, it involves modeling a growth mindset and a willingness to learn and improve. When parents acknowledge their mistakes or shortcomings with honesty and self-compassion, they demonstrate the healthy way to handle setbacks and failures. This approach can help children develop resilience and a willingness to take risks, knowing that mistakes are opportunities for growth.

Ultimately, when children witness their parents embodying the principles of mindfulness – emotional intelligence, effective communication, compassion, self-care, and a growth mindset – they are provided with a powerful blueprint for living a healthy, balanced, and fulfilling life. By serving as role models of these behaviors, mindful parents empower their children to develop the essential skills and mindsets necessary for thriving in all areas of life.

7. Greater Enjoyment of Parenting

While parenting is undoubtedly one of life's most rewarding experiences, it can also be incredibly demanding, stressful, and at times, overwhelming. In the midst of the daily grind of chores, tantrums, and schedules, it's easy for parents to lose sight of the magic and joy that lies at the heart of raising children. Mindful parenting offers a powerful antidote to this by encouraging parents to savor and appreciate the present moments they share with their children, cultivating a deeper sense of fulfillment and enjoyment in the parenting journey.

At its core, mindful parenting is about being fully present and engaged in each moment, rather than allowing the mind to dwell on the past or worry about the future. By anchoring their attention in the here and now, parents can truly appreciate the fleeting but precious experiences that accompany raising children – the belly laughs, the spontaneous hugs, the wide-eyed wonder, and the heartfelt connections that so often get overshadowed by the busyness of daily life.

Mindfulness practices, such as meditation and mindful breathing, help parents cultivate this present-moment awareness by training the mind to let go of distracting thoughts and fully immerse themselves in the current experience. This heightened sense of presence allows parents to notice and cherish the small, seemingly insignificant moments that might otherwise be missed, such as the way their child's eyes light up when they learn something new or the feeling of their tiny hand clasped in theirs.

Moreover, mindful parenting encourages parents to approach each moment with a sense of curiosity, openness, and non-judgment. Rather than reacting automatically to challenges or viewing them as burdens, mindful parents can choose to embrace the unpredictability and messiness of parenting as opportunities for growth, connection, and even humor. This shift in perspective can transform seemingly mundane or frustrating experiences into sources of joy and appreciation.

By savoring the present moments and cultivating a non-judgmental attitude, mindful parents are also better equipped to let go of unrealistic expectations or self-criticism. They can more readily accept the imperfections and challenges that are inherent in parenting, freeing themselves from the constant striving for an idealized version of parenthood and instead embracing the authentic, messy, and beautiful reality of raising children.

Ultimately, greater enjoyment and fulfillment in parenting have far-reaching benefits for both parents and children. When parents approach their role with a sense of presence, appreciation, and joy, they create a warm, nurturing environment that supports their child's emotional and cognitive development. Additionally, by modeling a mindful, present-focused approach to life, parents instill valuable lessons about living with intention, gratitude, and mindfulness – lessons that can serve their children well throughout their lives.

Mindful parenting offers a pathway to rediscovering the inherent joy and magic of raising children, even amidst the chaos and demands of daily life. By savoring each moment, embracing imperfection, and cultivating a sense of appreciation, parents can experience greater fulfillment and enjoyment in the parenting journey, creating cherished memories and fostering a deeper connection with their children along the way.

Common Challenges to Mindfulness and How to Overcome Them

There are certain common challenges to mindfulness for parents and usually make parenting a hurdle however there are also ways of how to overcome them:

1. Self-Judgment and Lack of Self-Compassion

As parents, we often hold ourselves to impossibly high standards, berating ourselves for perceived failures or moments when we fall short of our idealized version of the "perfect parent." This harsh inner critic can be a formidable barrier to mindful parenting, as it perpetuates stress, negativity, and a lack of self-acceptance – directly contradicting the principles of non-judgment and compassion that are central to mindfulness.

The Challenge:

Self-judgment often stems from deeply ingrained beliefs and societal pressures that tell us we must be flawless caregivers, always patient, nurturing, and in control. When we inevitably make mistakes, react impulsively, or struggle with the demands of parenting, our inner critic is quick to pounce, labeling us as "bad parents" or telling us we're not doing enough for our children.

This relentless self-criticism can lead to a vicious cycle of guilt, shame, and self-doubt, further depleting our emotional resources and making it even harder to show up for our children with presence and compassion. Moreover, when we judge ourselves harshly, we model that same harsh, critical voice for our children, potentially setting them up to internalize those negative thought patterns themselves.

<u>Overcoming the Challenge:</u>

To break free from the grip of self-judgment and create space for mindful parenting, we must cultivate self-compassion – the ability to treat ourselves with kindness, understanding, and forgiveness, just as we would a dear friend or loved one.

Self-compassion begins with recognizing that imperfection, struggles, and setbacks are an inherent part of the shared human experience. We are not alone in our challenges, and our worth as parents and individuals is not contingent on meeting unrealistic standards of perfection. By acknowledging our common humanity, we can begin to soften our inner critic and embrace ourselves with greater acceptance and compassion.

Practical exercises for building self-compassion include:

❖ Talking to ourselves with kindness and understanding when we make mistakes or feel overwhelmed, using the same gentle tone and words we would use to comfort a friend in our situation.

❖ Practicing self-forgiveness through affirmations, mantras, or journaling exercises that reinforce our innate worthiness and the inevitability of imperfection.

❖ Visualizing how we would comfort and encourage a dear friend who is struggling with the same challenges we face as parents, then directing that same compassion inward.

❖ Seeking support and validation from other compassionate parents, support groups, or a therapist who can provide an empathetic, non-judgmental space to process our experiences and emotions.

By embracing self-compassion, we create the emotional safety and self-acceptance necessary to fully embody the principles of mindful parenting. When we treat ourselves with kindness and understanding, we model those same qualities for our children, fostering an environment of emotional intelligence, resilience, and unconditional love.

2. Unrealistic Expectations and Attachment to Outcomes

In the journey of parenting, it's all too easy to become attached to specific visions or expectations about how our children should behave, develop, or achieve. We may have preconceived notions about developmental milestones, academic performance, or even personality traits that we hope our children will embody. However, when reality inevitably deviates from these rigid expectations, we can find ourselves feeling disappointed, frustrated, or even like failures as parents.

The Challenge:

Clinging to unrealistic expectations and attachment to specific outcomes directly conflicts with the core mindfulness principles of acceptance, non-judgment, and present-moment awareness. When we fixate on how things "should" be, rather than embracing the reality of how they are, we close ourselves off from the richness and beauty of the present moment.

This attachment can manifest in various ways:

❖ Frustration when our children don't meet developmental milestones at the "expected" ages

❖ Disappointment or disapproval when our children's personalities or interests don't align with our desires

❖ Excessive focus on academic or extracurricular achievement, at the expense of emotional wellbeing

❖ Rigidity in how we believe our children should behave or express themselves

Not only does this attachment to expectations breed stress and negativity for parents, but it can also have detrimental effects on our children. When we project our own agendas or visions onto them, we risk undermining their sense of autonomy, self-acceptance, and intrinsic motivation.

Overcoming the Challenge:

To embrace mindful parenting fully, we must learn to let go of unrealistic expectations and attachment to specific outcomes. This involves cultivating a profound sense of acceptance and flexibility, recognizing that every child is a unique individual who will develop and thrive at their own pace, in their own way.

Here are some strategies to help shift our perspective:

❖ Radical Acceptance: Fully embracing our children and ourselves as we are, without condition. This involves letting go of preconceived notions and celebrating the inherent beauty and potential in each stage of our children's development.

❖ Reframing Challenges: Instead of viewing struggles or setbacks as failures, we can choose to reframe them as opportunities for growth, learning, and deepening our connection with our children. Every challenge holds the potential for wisdom and resilience.

❖ Focusing on the Present Moment: Rather than fixating on future outcomes or comparing our children to arbitrary standards, we can shift our attention to the present-moment experience of connecting with and nurturing our children's unique gifts and needs.

❖ Embracing a Growth Mindset: Recognizing that our children (and we ourselves) are constantly evolving and capable of change and growth, regardless of perceived limitations or setbacks.

By letting go of rigid expectations and attachment to outcomes, we create space for true presence, acceptance, and unconditional love in our relationships with our children. We can fully appreciate and savor each moment, without the weight of unfulfilled expectations or disappointment clouding our experiences. In doing so, we model resilience, self-acceptance, and a growth mindset that will serve our children well throughout their lives.

3. Dealing with Parental Guilt

Parenting is a journey rife with challenges, emotions, and inevitable missteps. Even the most devoted and mindful parents will make mistakes or have moments where they fall short of their own standards or expectations. However, many parents struggle to move past these perceived failures, instead becoming mired in overwhelming feelings of guilt and self-reproach.

The Challenge:

Parental guilt can stem from a variety of sources – losing one's patience and raising our voice, missing an important event or milestone, failing to provide the "perfect" childhood experience, or simply feeling that we haven't lived up to our own idealized vision of what it means to be a "good parent." This guilt can be exacerbated by societal pressures, unrealistic expectations, and the constant comparisons that are so prevalent in today's parenting culture.

When left unchecked, parental guilt can become a formidable obstacle to mindful parenting. It can lead to rumination over past mistakes, sapping our energy and presence in the current moment. It can breed resentment, self-criticism, and a lack of self-compassion, making it even harder to show up for our children with patience, acceptance, and emotional intelligence.

Overcoming the Challenge:

To move beyond the weight of parental guilt, we must first acknowledge that making mistakes is an inevitable and essential part of the learning process – for both ourselves and our children. Perfection is an unattainable and ultimately unhelpful standard, and striving for it often comes at the expense of our own well-being and our ability to be fully present with our children.

Instead, we can embrace a growth mindset, recognizing that every misstep or challenge presents an opportunity for growth, self-reflection, and deepening our understanding of ourselves and our children.

Here are some strategies for dealing with parental guilt in a mindful, self-compassionate way:

❖ Practice Self-Forgiveness: When we make mistakes or fall short of our own expectations, we must treat ourselves with the same kindness and forgiveness we would extend to a dear friend. We can use affirmations, journaling, or visualization exercises to actively cultivate self-forgiveness and release the grip of guilt.

❖ Let Go of Perfection: Acknowledge that perfection is an unrealistic and ultimately counterproductive goal. Instead, strive for progress, not perfection, and celebrate the small victories and moments of connection that arise amidst the challenges.

❖ Focus on the Present Moment: Rather than dwelling on past regrets or future worries, anchor ourselves in the present moment through mindfulness practices like deep breathing or body scans. This present-moment awareness allows us to show up for our children with greater clarity, patience, and emotional availability.

❖ Make Amends When Necessary: If we have truly made a mistake that has impacted our children, take responsibility and make sincere efforts to repair the relationship or situation. However, avoid excessive self-flagellation or dwelling on the past once amends have been made.

❖ Seek Support: Connect with other parents, join support groups, or seek professional guidance to process feelings of guilt and self-doubt in a healthy, constructive manner. Having a compassionate and non-judgmental space to share our experiences can be incredibly healing.

By addressing parental guilt with self-compassion, mindfulness, and a growth mindset, we can release ourselves from the weight of unrealistic expectations and past regrets. This freedom allows us to show up for our children with greater presence, emotional intelligence, and unconditional love, fostering a nurturing and supportive environment for their growth and development.

4. Overwhelm, Stress, and Lack of Time

In the whirlwind of modern parenting, with its endless demands, responsibilities, and distractions, it can feel almost impossible to carve out time and mental space for mindfulness practices. The constant juggling of work, household chores, extracurricular activities, and the ever-present needs of our children can leave parents feeling overwhelmed, stressed, and perpetually rushed – states that are antithetical to the present-moment awareness and inner calm that mindfulness cultivates.

The Challenge:

When we're in a constant state of overwhelm and busyness, our minds become fragmented, jumping from one task to the next without ever truly being present for any of them. We may find ourselves going through the motions of parenting, but lacking the emotional availability, patience, and connection that our children crave.

This chronic stress and lack of presence can have far-reaching consequences for both parents and children. It can lead to burnout, emotional exhaustion, and a sense of disconnection or resentment towards the very experiences and relationships that should bring us joy and fulfillment.

For children, growing up in an environment of parental overwhelm and inattention can contribute to feelings of insecurity, emotional dysregulation, and a lack of role modeling for healthy stress management and self-care.

While the demands of parenting can indeed be overwhelming at times, it's crucial that we prioritize self-care and find creative ways to integrate mindfulness into our daily routines. By doing so, we can cultivate the inner resources and resilience necessary to navigate the chaos with greater grace, presence, and emotional intelligence.

Here are some strategies to help overcome the challenge of overwhelm and lack of time:

❖ Schedule Regular "Mindful Breaks": Even just a few minutes of mindful breathing, meditation, or body scans throughout the day can help reset our minds and bodies, reducing stress and promoting present-moment awareness.

❖ Practice Mindfulness During Routine Activities: Rather than viewing tasks like washing dishes, folding laundry, or bathing children as chores, we can transform them into opportunities for mindfulness by bringing our full attention to the sensory experiences and present-moment unfolding of these activities.

❖ Involve Children in Mindfulness Activities: Simple practices like breathing exercises, nature walks, or mindful coloring can not only help manage our own stress but also introduce our children to the benefits of mindfulness from an early age.

❖ Seek Support and Create Spaciousness: Enlist the help of partners, friends, or family members to create pockets of personal time for self-care and mindfulness practices. Even small chunks of time can be profoundly restorative.

❖ Reframe Unavoidable Stressors: Instead of resisting or becoming overwhelmed by the inevitable challenges of parenting, we can choose to view them as opportunities to practice present-moment awareness, emotional regulation, and resilience.

By making mindfulness and self-care priorities, even amidst the busyness of parenting, we not only cultivate our own well-being but also model invaluable lessons for our children about stress management, work-life balance, and the importance of nurturing our emotional and spiritual selves alongside our many responsibilities.

BONUS CHALLENGES:

5. Difficulty Letting Go of Multitasking and Distraction:

The Challenge:

Our digital age thrives on multitasking and constant stimulation. Parents often find themselves checking phones, responding to emails, or completing chores while attempting to interact with their children. This fragmented attention hinders present-moment focus and connection, crucial elements for fostering emotional intelligence in children.

Overcoming the Challenge:

The key lies in cultivating habits of single-tasking and mindful presence when interacting with children. Here are some strategies:

❖ Embrace Single-Tasking: Shift your mindset away from multitasking. Instead, focus on completing one task at a time with your full attention. While playing with your child, put away your phone and resist the urge to check emails. Dedicate that time to being fully present in the activity.

❖ Create Tech-Free Zones: Establish specific times and spaces within the day where technology is off-limits. This could be during mealtimes, bedtime routines, or designated play sessions with your children. This allows for focused interaction and fosters deeper connection.

❖ Simplify Schedules: Overfilled schedules can contribute to feeling overwhelmed and resorting to multitasking. Review your family calendar and identify areas for simplification. Can certain activities be combined or rescheduled? Delegate tasks where possible, and prioritize quality time with your children over packed schedules.

❖ Model Focused Attention: Children learn by observing their parents. Demonstrate focused attention by actively engaging in activities with your child. Listen attentively when they speak, ask open-ended questions, and make eye contact. This teaches them the importance of presence and fosters healthy communication habits.

❖ Mindfulness Practices: Integrate mindfulness practices into your daily routine. This can include short meditation sessions, mindful breathing exercises, or even mindful walks together as a family. By cultivating your own awareness, you become better equipped to teach your children about managing distractions and remaining present in the moment.

By prioritizing focused attention and mindful presence, you can build stronger connections with your children, creating a foundation for emotional intelligence and a more fulfilling parent-child relationship.

6. Difficulty Managing Strong Emotions:

The Challenge:

Parenting inevitably triggers strong emotions. From frustration during tantrums to worry about your child's safety, these intense feelings can hijack our ability to respond mindfully. When emotions escalate, it becomes difficult to connect with our children and model healthy emotional regulation.

Overcoming the Challenge:

The key to managing strong emotions in the parenting context lies in developing your emotional regulation toolkit and seeking support when needed. Here are some strategies:

❖ Mindful Breathing: When you feel overwhelmed by emotions, pause and practice mindful breathing exercises. Focus on your breath, inhaling slowly and deeply, and exhaling completely. This simple technique helps calm the nervous system and allows you to regain a sense of composure before responding.

❖ Body Awareness: Pay attention to your physical sensations when emotions begin to rise. Do you feel tightness in your chest? Clenched fists? Tuning into body signals can serve as an early warning system, prompting you to employ calming strategies before your emotions escalate.

❖ Self-Compassion: Acknowledge your emotional experience with self-compassion. It's normal to feel frustrated or overwhelmed as a parent. Instead of harsh self-criticism, offer yourself understanding. Say to yourself, "It's okay to feel this way right now. I can handle this."

❖ Time-Outs for Parents: Just like children, sometimes parents need a time-out. If you feel your emotions bubbling over, excuse yourself from the situation momentarily. Take a few deep breaths, splash some water on your face, or practice a relaxation technique. Returning to the situation calmer allows for a more mindful response.

❖ Seek Support: Don't hesitate to seek support from your partner, family, friends, or a therapist. Talking about your challenges and experiences can ease the burden and offer valuable perspectives. Sometimes, simply expressing your emotions can be a form of emotional release and lead to calmer reactions.

Remember, your children are constantly learning from your behavior. By managing your own emotions mindfully, you model healthy coping mechanisms and equip them with essential tools to navigate their own emotional landscape effectively.

7. Dealing with Parental Burnout:

The Challenge:

The relentless demands of parenting can lead to burnout, leaving parents feeling emotionally drained, exhausted, and overwhelmed. In this depleted state, it becomes incredibly difficult to be present and patient with your children, hindering the very connection you strive for. The constant pressure to meet unrealistic expectations, coupled with the sleep deprivation, and the juggle of work and family life can create a perfect storm for burnout.

Overcoming the Challenge:

The key to overcoming parental burnout lies in a two-pronged approach: prioritizing self-care and building a strong support system. Here are some strategies to get you back on track:

❖ Recognize the Signs: Familiarize yourself with the early signs of burnout. These can include chronic fatigue, irritability, withdrawal from loved ones, difficulty concentrating, feelings of hopelessness, and increased reliance on unhealthy coping mechanisms like emotional eating or substance abuse. By recognizing the early signs, you can take proactive steps to address them before burnout takes hold.

❖ Prioritize Self-Care: Self-care is not a luxury - it's essential for sustainable parenting. Integrate activities that promote relaxation and rejuvenation into your routine, even if it's just small pockets of time throughout the day. This could include meditation, exercise, spending time in nature, or pursuing hobbies you enjoy. Prioritizing activities that nourish your soul allows you to replenish your emotional reserves and return to parenting with renewed energy. Consider activities that bring you joy and a sense of accomplishment, whether it's reading a book, taking a relaxing bath, or spending time with friends.

By prioritizing self-care, building a strong support system, and recognizing the signs of burnout, you can prevent it from derailing your parenting journey and ensure you have the emotional resources to nurture your children and foster their emotional intelligence. Remember, a well-rested and supported parent is a better parent. Taking care of yourself is the foundation for raising emotionally intelligent children.

Chapter 3: Building Your Mindful Toolkit

Mindfulness Practices for Parents

1. Meditation:

Meditation might conjure images of sitting cross-legged for hours, but the reality is far simpler. Meditation is essentially about training your attention and cultivating present-moment awareness. Here are some beginner-friendly meditation techniques:

❖ **Mindfulness of Breath Meditation:** This foundational practice involves focusing your attention on your breath. Find a quiet spot, close your eyes (if comfortable), and feel your breath entering and leaving your body. When your mind wanders (and it will!), gently bring your attention back to your breath without judgment. Start with just a few minutes a day and gradually increase the duration as you become more comfortable.

❖ **Body Scan Meditation:** This practice invites you to tune into your bodily sensations. Lie down comfortably or sit in a relaxed posture. Close your eyes and begin by focusing on your toes. Notice any sensations of tension, relaxation, warmth, or coolness. Gradually work your way up your body, focusing on each major muscle group with a gentle, non-judgmental awareness.

❖ **Guided Meditations:** Numerous guided meditations are available online or through apps. These meditations provide gentle prompts and instructions to guide your attention and focus on specific themes like calming the mind, fostering compassion, or promoting gratitude.

While meditation is often depicted as a solitary practice requiring hours of undisturbed silence, the reality for parents is far more practical. Here's how to cultivate a meditation practice that fits seamlessly into your busy life, even with just a few stolen moments throughout the day:

1. Mindfulness of Breath Meditation:

This foundational technique is a powerful tool for anchoring yourself in the present moment. Here's a step-by-step guide to get you started:

❖ **Embrace the Short Sessions:** Instead of aiming for a mythical hour of uninterrupted meditation, focus on achievable micro-meditations. Even five minutes of mindful breathing can significantly reduce stress and improve focus. Sneak these mini-sessions in throughout your day: while your coffee brews, waiting for the laundry to finish, or during a short break between errands.

❖ **Transform Your Commute:** If you drive, use your commute as an opportunity for mindfulness. Focus on the rhythm of your breath and the sensations in your body as you navigate traffic. If you use public transportation, close your eyes (if safe) and practice a few minutes of mindful breathing.

❖ **Make Use of Waiting Periods:** Those inevitable moments of waiting in line, at the doctor's office, or for your child's pick-up can be mini-meditation opportunities. Close your eyes, take a few deep breaths, and focus on the present moment, letting go of anxieties about the past or future.

2. Body Scan Meditation:

This practice invites you to cultivate awareness of your body and release any physical tension you might be holding. Here's how to experience a body scan meditation:

❖ **Start with Progressive Muscle Relaxation (Optional):** Before your body scan, consider incorporating a few minutes of progressive muscle relaxation. Tense and release different muscle groups throughout your body, starting with your toes and working your way up. This can help release accumulated tension and prepare you for a deeper body scan.

❖ **Bring Awareness to Your Breath:** After your progressive muscle relaxation (or if you choose to skip it), take a few moments to focus on your breath. This helps ground you in the present moment and prepares your mind for the body scan.

❖ **Expand Your Awareness Beyond Physical Sensations:** As you scan your body, pay attention not just to physical sensations but also to any emotions or thoughts that arise. Acknowledge them without judgment and gently guide your attention back to the body scan.

❖ **End with Gratitude (or Loving-Kindness):** Once you've completed the body scan, take a few moments to cultivate gratitude for your body. You can also extend loving-kindness to yourself by silently wishing yourself well-being and peace.

3. Guided Meditations:

Guided meditations offer a fantastic resource for busy parents. These audio recordings provide gentle instructions and prompts to guide your attention and focus on specific themes. Here are some tips for using guided meditations effectively:

❖ **Explore Different Apps and Instructors:** With a vast selection of meditation apps and online resources available, take some time to explore and find what works for you. Try different instructors, themes, and meditation lengths to discover what resonates most with your preferences.

❖ **Create a Supportive Environment:** When possible, find a quiet space to listen to your guided meditation, free from distractions. Dim the lights, put your phone on silent, and create a comfortable setting that allows you to fully immerse yourself in the experience.

❖ **Meditation Doesn't Have to Be Perfect:** Don't get discouraged if your mind wanders during guided meditation. It's natural for thoughts to arise. The key is to gently guide your attention back to the recording without judgment.

❖ **Meditation is a Practice:** Like any skill, meditation takes practice. The more you integrate it into your routine, the more comfortable and effective it will become. Be patient with yourself and celebrate your progress along the way. By incorporating these mindfulness practices into your daily life, you can cultivate greater self-awareness, manage stress more effectively, and create a more peaceful and connected environment for yourself and your children.

2. Breathing Exercises:

Our breath is a powerful tool for regulating emotions and promoting relaxation. Here are two simple breathing exercises you can practice throughout the day:

❖ **Diaphragmatic Breathing (Belly Breathing):** Sit or lie down comfortably. Place one hand on your chest and the other on your belly. Breathe in slowly and deeply through your nose, feeling your belly inflate (not your chest). Exhale slowly and completely through pursed lips. Practice this for a few minutes, focusing on the calming rhythm of your breath.

❖ **4-7-8 Breathing:** This calming technique involves inhaling through your nose for a count of four, holding your breath for a count of seven, and exhaling completely through your mouth for a count of eight. Repeat this cycle several times to experience a sense of relaxation and focus.

Even amidst the whirlwind of parenthood, your breath remains a powerful and accessible tool for managing stress and promoting relaxation. Here's a deeper dive into two effective breathing exercises you can integrate seamlessly into your daily routine, along with some tips on incorporating them into your life as a busy parent:

1. Diaphragmatic Breathing (Belly Breathing):

This fundamental technique activates your diaphragm, the muscle that separates your chest cavity from your abdomen. Belly breathing promotes relaxation by stimulating the parasympathetic nervous system, your body's rest-and-digest response. Here's how to master belly breathing:

❖ **Finding Your Anchor:** Sit or lie down comfortably in a position that allows your belly to expand freely. You can place one hand on your chest and the other on your belly to feel the movement during the exercise. If you're sitting, avoid slouching and ensure your spine is relatively straight for optimal breath control.

❖ **The Inhale:** Imagine you're inflating a balloon with your belly, not your chest. Breathe in slowly and deeply through your nose for a count of four. Feel your belly push outwards against your hand as you inhale.

❖ **The Exhale:** Once your belly is comfortably full, purse your lips slightly and exhale slowly and completely through your mouth for a count of six. Feel your belly flatten as you exhale, engaging your core muscles.

❖ **Finding Your Rhythm:** Focus on the natural rhythm of your breath. Aim for a smooth, controlled inhale followed by a slow, complete exhale. Don't force your breath, and if you experience any dizziness, simply slow down the counting or shorten the exercise.

❖ **Practice Makes Perfect:** Start with short practice sessions of 3-5 minutes. Gradually increase the duration as you become more comfortable. Aim to incorporate diaphragmatic breathing throughout your day, whenever you feel overwhelmed or stressed. Try belly breathing while waiting in line, during a short break between errands, or while folding laundry.

2. 4-7-8 Breathing:

This calming technique offers a quick and effective way to de-escalate emotions and promote focus. When practiced regularly, it can also improve sleep quality. Here's a step-by-step guide:

❖ **Finding Your Center:** Sit comfortably with your back straight and shoulders relaxed. Close your eyes gently if that feels comfortable.

❖ **The Inhale:** Inhale slowly and silently through your nose for a count of four. Visualize drawing calming energy up from your core with each inhale.

❖ **The Hold:** Hold your breath for a count of seven, but avoid straining. Imagine suspending that peaceful energy within you.

❖ **The Release:** Exhale completely through your mouth for a count of eight, making a whooshing sound as if you're deflating a balloon. Release any tension or worries you might be holding onto with this exhale.

❖ **Repeating for Relaxation:** Repeat this cycle of inhaling for four, holding for seven, and exhaling for eight for several rounds (typically 4-8 cycles) until you feel a sense of calm wash over you.

Transforming Your Day with Breathwork:

❖ **Beat the Morning Rush:** Start your day with a few minutes of diaphragmatic breathing to energize yourself and promote focus for the day ahead. As you breathe in, imagine inhaling positive intentions for the day, and as you exhale, release any anxieties or worries that might be lingering.

❖ **Navigate Tantrums with Calmness:** When faced with a child's meltdown, excuse yourself for a moment and take a few rounds of 4-7-8 breaths to regain your composure before responding. Stepping away for a minute to collect yourself, while utilizing calming breaths, allows you to approach the situation with more patience and understanding.

❖ **Transform Bedtime with Relaxation:** Incorporate calming belly breaths into your bedtime routine to help yourself and your child wind down and prepare for a restful night's sleep. Cuddle with your child and practice belly breaths together, creating a sense of peace and security before lights out.

Remember, incorporating mindful breathing practices into your daily routine empowers you to manage stress effectively, fostering a calmer and more present experience of parenthood. By making these exercises a habit, you'll equip yourself with powerful tools to navigate the inevitable challenges of parenthood with greater ease and self-compassion.

3. Mindful Listening:

Truly listening to your children goes beyond simply hearing their words. It's about giving them your full attention and creating a safe space for them to express themselves freely. Here's how to cultivate mindful listening:

❖ **Put Away Distractions:** Silence your phone, turn off the TV, and make eye contact with your child when they're speaking.

❖ **Focus on Understanding:** Listen with the intent to understand, not to react or judge.

❖ **Ask Open-Ended Questions:** Instead of yes or no questions, encourage elaboration with prompts like "Tell me more about that" or "How did that make you feel?"

❖ **Validate Their Emotions:** Acknowledge their feelings, even if you don't agree with them. Say things like "It sounds like you're feeling frustrated" or "I understand why you might be upset."

Truly listening to your children is the foundation for a strong and connected parent-child relationship. It fosters trust, understanding, and creates a safe space for them to express themselves openly and honestly. However, amidst the constant demands of parenthood, truly listening can feel like a luxury. Here's a breakdown of mindful listening practices you can integrate into your daily interactions with your children, even when time feels scarce:

1. Create a Calming and Focused Environment:

❖ **Minimize Distractions:** Before engaging with your child, silence your phone, turn off the TV, and put away any other distractions. This demonstrates that their conversation has your full and undivided attention.

❖ **Make Eye Contact:** Look into your child's eyes and hold their gaze in a warm and inviting way. Eye contact conveys genuine interest and encourages them to elaborate.

❖ **Get Down to Their Level:** When possible, physically get down to your child's eye level. This creates a sense of equality and psychological safety, making them feel more comfortable opening up.

2. Be Present in the Moment:

❖ **Put Worries Aside:** Acknowledge any worries or anxieties swirling in your mind, but gently place them on hold while you focus on your child.

❖ **Listen with Your Heart:** Pay attention not just to their words, but also to their emotional tone and body language. Notice any nonverbal cues that might indicate underlying emotions.

❖ **Practice Active Listening:** Briefly paraphrase what you hear to ensure understanding. This shows you're paying attention and encourages them to continue sharing.

3. Encourage Elaboration:

❖ **Ask Open-Ended Questions:** Instead of questions with yes or no answers, prompt them to elaborate with questions like "Tell me more about what happened at school today" or "How did that situation make you feel?"

❖ **Avoid Interrupting:** Allow them to finish their thoughts before responding. Patience is key in creating a safe space for open communication.

❖ **Embrace Silence:** Don't feel pressured to fill every silence with words. Sometimes, comfortable silences allow your child to process their thoughts and emotions before continuing.

4. Validate Their Feelings:

❖ **Acknowledge Their Emotions:** Let your child know that their feelings are valid, even if you don't necessarily agree with them. Phrases like "It sounds like you're feeling frustrated" or "I understand why you might be upset" show empathy and create a safe space for emotional expression.

❖ **Focus on Understanding, Not Fixing:** Don't jump in with solutions or try to minimize their feelings. The goal is to understand their perspective and create a space where they feel heard and supported.

❖ **Offer Comfort and Support:** Once they've expressed themselves, offer words of comfort, support, and guidance, if appropriate.

Mindful listening is a journey, not a destination. There will be times when you're pulled in a million directions, and focused listening might feel challenging. Be patient with yourself, and celebrate your efforts to connect with your child on a deeper level. By incorporating these practices into your daily interactions, you'll cultivate a stronger bond, build trust, and foster a safe space for open communication with your children.

4. Mindful Communication:

Mindful communication involves expressing yourself clearly and calmly, while considering the impact on your child. Here are some tips:

❖ **"I" Statements:** Use "I" statements to express your needs and feelings without blaming or criticizing your child. For example, "I feel frustrated when my toys are left out" instead of "You always leave your toys everywhere!"

❖ **Active Listening:** Before responding, paraphrase what you heard to ensure understanding. This shows you're paying attention and encourages them to elaborate.

❖ **Focus on Positive Reinforcement:** Catch your child being good! Acknowledge and praise positive behaviors to encourage them further.

❖ **Use a Calm and Soothing Tone:** Even if you're feeling frustrated, maintaining a calm and respectful tone can de-escalate situations and promote open communication.

Mindful communication is the cornerstone of a healthy parent-child relationship. It's about expressing yourself clearly and calmly, while considering the impact your words have on your child. Here's a deeper dive into mindful communication practices you can incorporate into your daily interactions:

1. Speak from "I"

❖ **"I" Statements vs. Blaming:** Instead of accusatory statements that put your child on the defensive (e.g., "You always leave your toys everywhere!"), use "I" statements to express how their actions make you feel. For example, "I feel frustrated when my toys are left out because it makes it hard to clean up."

❖ **Focus on Feelings:** "I" statements help your child understand the impact of their behavior on your emotions, fostering empathy and encouraging them to consider your perspective.

2. Active Listening: Building Understanding

❖ **Paraphrase and Reflect:** Before responding, paraphrase what you heard to ensure understanding. This shows you're paying attention and validates their experience. You can say things like, "So it sounds like you're feeling frustrated because..." or "If I understand correctly, you were..."

❖ **Ask Clarifying Questions:** If something is unclear, ask open-ended questions to encourage elaboration. This demonstrates your genuine interest in their perspective and helps you address the root of the issue.

3. Positive Reinforcement: Encouraging Good Behavior

❖ **Catch Them Being Good:** Don't just point out negative behaviors. Acknowledge and praise your child's positive actions and choices. This reinforces good behavior and motivates them to continue making positive choices.

❖ **Be Specific with Praise:** Instead of generic praise, highlight specific actions you appreciate. For example, "Thank you for helping me clean up your toys. That was a big help!" Specific praise shows them exactly what behaviors you value.

4. Speak with Calmness and Respect:

❖ **Stay Calm:** Even when you're feeling frustrated, avoid raising your voice or using harsh language. Taking a deep breath and calming yourself down allows for a more productive conversation.

❖ **Focus on Problem-Solving:** Approach situations as opportunities to problem-solve together. Discuss the issue, brainstorm solutions, and work collaboratively to find a solution that works for everyone.

Mindful communication is an ongoing practice. There will be times when you misstep, and that's okay. The key is to apologize when necessary, learn from your mistakes, and strive to connect with your child in a respectful and understanding way. By incorporating these practices into your daily interactions, you'll cultivate a stronger bond with your child, build trust, and create a safe space for open communication

5. Practice Gratitude:

Cultivating a daily gratitude practice can shift parents' focus from stress and worry to appreciation and abundance. Encourage parents to reflect on three things they are grateful for each day, whether it's a small moment of joy with their child, a supportive friend, or a moment of peace amidst the chaos. Practicing gratitude can foster a positive mindset and deepen the parent-child connection. Here are some ways to incorporate gratitude into your routine:

❖ **Start a Gratitude Journal:** Dedicate a few minutes each day to write down three things you're grateful for.

❖ **Share Gratitude at Mealtimes:** During mealtimes, take turns sharing one thing each person is grateful for that day.

❖ **Create a Gratitude Jar:** Decorate a...jar and write down things you're grateful for on small pieces of paper. Fold them up and add them to the jar. Over time, you can revisit these moments of gratitude

Gratitude isn't just a feel-good practice; it's a powerful tool that can significantly enhance your parenting experience. By cultivating an attitude of gratitude, you can shift your focus from the daily stresses to the countless blessings inherent in parenthood. Here's a deeper exploration of gratitude practices you can easily integrate into your routine, fostering a more positive and joyful experience for yourself and your children:

1. Cultivating a Gratitude Mindset:

❖ **Shifting Focus:** Our brains naturally tend to focus on negative stimuli. Mindful gratitude practice counters this by intentionally shifting your focus towards appreciating the positive aspects of your life, big or small.

❖ **Appreciating the Little Things:** Take time to savor the simple joys of parenthood: a child's laughter, a warm cuddle, a moment of shared creativity. These seemingly small moments are the building blocks of precious memories.

2. Gratitude Journaling for Reflection:

❖ **Daily Reflections:** Dedicate a few minutes each day, perhaps first thing in the morning or before bed, to write down three things you're grateful for. This could be anything from your child's health to a supportive partner, a good night's sleep, or a moment of peace amidst the chaos.

❖ **Reflecting on Growth:** As you review your gratitude journal entries over time, you can witness your own growth and appreciate the positive changes in your life and your child's development.

3. Sharing Gratitude: Connecting with Your Child

❖ **Mealtime Gratitude:** Turn mealtimes into opportunities to connect and cultivate gratitude. Start a tradition where each person shares one thing they're grateful for that day.

❖ **Gratitude Games:** Make gratitude fun and engaging through games. Play "I Spy Gratitude," taking turns finding things to appreciate in your environment. You can also create a gratitude scavenger hunt, with clues leading to hidden notes expressing things you're grateful for about your child.

4. Creating Tangible Reminders: The Gratitude Jar

❖ **A Visual Representation:** Decorate a jar and turn it into a tangible reminder of your blessings. Throughout the day, write down on small pieces of paper things you're grateful for: a funny moment with your child, a kind gesture from a friend, a personal accomplishment.

❖ **Revisiting Your Blessings:** Periodically, revisit your gratitude jar as a family. Read aloud the notes, reminiscing about the positive experiences and emotions they represent.

Gratitude is a practice, not a destination. There will be days when negativity creeps in. Be patient with yourself and recommit to cultivating an attitude of appreciation. By incorporating these practices into your daily routine, you'll foster a more positive and joyful parenting experience, not just for yourself, but for your children as well. A grateful parent raises a grateful child, and together you can build a foundation of positivity and appreciation for life's simple joys.

6. Mindful Movement:

Engaging in mindful movement practices such as yoga, tai chi, or simply taking a mindful walk in nature can help parents reconnect with their bodies, reduce stress, and cultivate presence. Encourage parents to incorporate mindful movement into their daily routines, whether through a structured class or integrating mindful movement into everyday activities such as stretching or walking with their children. Here are some tips for mindful movement:

❖ **Focus on Your Body:** Pay attention to the physical sensations in your body as you move. Feel the ground beneath your feet, the stretch in your muscles, and the rhythm of your breath.

❖ **Move with Intention:** Avoid going through the motions mindlessly. Be present in each movement, whether it's folding laundry or playing tag with your child.

❖ **Find Activities You Enjoy:** Choose activities you find pleasurable and sustainable. This could be anything from dancing to gardening to playing a sport.

❖ **Start Small:** You don't need to dedicate hours to mindful movement. Begin with short bursts of activity throughout the day, gradually increasing the duration as you become more comfortable

The constant demands of parenthood can leave you feeling disconnected from your own body. Mindful movement practices offer a powerful antidote, promoting stress reduction, increased self-awareness, and a deeper connection to the present moment. Here's a deeper exploration of mindful movement practices you can integrate into your daily routine, even amidst the whirlwind of parenthood:

1. Reconnecting with Your Body Through Movement:

❖ **Focus on Bodily Sensations:** Mindful movement isn't just about exercise; it's about cultivating awareness of your physical being. As you move, pay attention to the sensations in your body. Feel the ground beneath your feet, the stretch in your muscles, the rise and fall of your chest with each breath.

❖ **Moving with Intention:** Avoid going through the motions mindlessly. Instead, be present in each movement, big or small. Whether you're folding laundry, playing tag with your child, or enjoying a walk in nature, bring your full attention to the physical experience.

2. Finding Joyful Movement: Activities You Love

❖ **Explore Different Activities:** The key to sustainable mindful movement is finding activities you genuinely enjoy. This could be anything from yoga or tai chi to dancing, gardening, or playing a sport. Explore different options and discover what resonates with you.

❖ **Embrace Movement Throughout the Day:** You don't need to dedicate hours to reap the benefits of mindful movement. Incorporate short bursts of activity throughout your day. Stretch while waiting for the kettle to boil, take mindful walks during breaks, or transform playtime with your child into a joyful exploration of movement.

3. Starting Small and Building Consistency:

❖ **Gentle Beginnings:** Don't overwhelm yourself with unrealistic goals. Begin with short, manageable sessions of mindful movement. Start with 5-10 minutes a day and gradually increase the duration as you become more comfortable.

❖ **Building a Sustainable Habit:** Consistency is key. Aim to incorporate mindful movement into your routine most days of the week, even if it's just for a short period. The cumulative effect of these small practices will significantly enhance your well-being.

Here are some additional tips to help you integrate mindful movement into your daily life as a parent:

❖ **Turn Chores into Mindful Movement:** Transform everyday activities like folding laundry, cleaning the house, or gardening into opportunities for mindful movement. Focus on your breath and body sensations as you complete your tasks.

❖ **Embrace Family Movement Time:** Schedule family walks, dance parties, or yoga sessions together. Moving your body with your child fosters connection, creates positive memories, and instills healthy habits in them from a young age.

❖ **Utilize Online Resources:** Numerous online resources offer guided mindful movement sessions specifically designed for busy parents. Explore these options to find something that fits your preferences and schedule.

Mindful movement is a journey, not a destination. There will be days when you struggle to find time or motivation. Be patient with yourself, celebrate your progress, and recommit to prioritizing your well-being. By incorporating mindful movement practices into your daily routine, you'll cultivate a deeper connection to your body, reduce stress, and create a more present and joyful experience of parenthood.

Integrating Mindfulness into Daily Routines

Morning Routine

The first moments of your day set the tone for everything that follows. By establishing a mindful morning routine, you can cultivate a sense of calm, focus, and intention that will carry you throughout the day's inevitable challenges. Here's a breakdown of key practices to integrate into your morning routine, transforming it from a rushed frenzy to a mindful and nourishing experience:

1. Setting a Mindful Intention:

❖ **Planting the Seeds of Positivity:** Before you even get out of bed, take a few moments to set an intention for the day. This intention acts as a guiding light, influencing your mindset and directing your focus.

❖ **Exploring Different Intentions:** Your intention can be anything that resonates with you. Here are some examples:

○ **Gratitude:** Intentions of gratitude cultivate a positive outlook and appreciation for the day ahead. You could silently repeat a mantra like "Today, I choose to be grateful for..." or focus on something specific you're looking forward to.

○ **Presence:** An intention of presence encourages you to be fully engaged in the present moment, reducing worries about the future or dwelling on the past.

○ **Patience:** If you know you have a busy day ahead, setting an intention of patience can equip you to handle challenges and frustrations with greater ease.

❖ **Repeating Your Intention:** Throughout the day, gently remind yourself of your chosen intention. This helps you stay centered and focused, even amidst the chaos.

2. Mindful Movement: Waking Up Your Body and Mind

❖ **Gentle Stretches for Body Awareness:** After setting your intention, ease your body out of sleep with gentle stretches. Focus on each movement, feeling the sensations in your muscles and joints as you lengthen and extend.

❖ **Yoga for Inner Peace:** If you have more time, consider incorporating a short yoga routine into your morning. Yoga poses not only improve flexibility and strength but also promote mindfulness and inner peace.

❖ **Moving with Intention:** Even simple activities like making your bed or walking to the bathroom can be opportunities for mindful movement. Focus on your breath and body sensations as you complete these tasks.

3. Mindful Eating: Savoring Your Breakfast

❖ **Breaking the Fast with Awareness:** Instead of rushing through breakfast, take time to savor each bite. Sit down at a table, free from distractions like phones or emails.

❖ **Engaging Your Senses:** Pay attention to the colors, textures, and smells of your food. Notice the different tastes as you chew and appreciate the nourishment your body is receiving.

❖ **Mindful Breakfast Choices:** Consider starting your day with a nutritious and energizing breakfast. Whole grains, fruits, vegetables, and lean proteins provide sustained energy and support your overall well-being.

4. Building a Sustainable Routine:

❖ **Start Small:** Don't overwhelm yourself by trying to overhaul your entire morning routine at once. Begin with small, manageable changes. Start with setting an intention, and gradually incorporate mindful movement and mindful eating as you become more comfortable.

❖ **Find What Works for You:** There's no one-size-fits-all approach to a mindful morning routine. Experiment and discover practices that resonate with you and fit seamlessly into your schedule.

❖ **Consistency is Key:** The true benefits of mindfulness come from consistent practice. Aim to incorporate these practices into your morning routine most days of the week, even if it's just for a few minutes. Over time, you'll cultivate a sense of calm, focus, and well-being that sets the stage for a mindful and fulfilling day.

By integrating these practices into your morning routine, you'll be well on your way to establishing a foundation of mindfulness that will enhance your parenting experience and enrich your life as a whole. Remember, mindfulness is a journey, not a destination. Be patient with yourself, celebrate your progress, and enjoy the process of creating a more mindful and present morning experience.

Throughout the Day

While a mindful morning routine sets the tone for the day, mindfulness isn't confined to the first few hours. By integrating mindful practices throughout your day, you can cultivate a sense of calm, focus, and presence in the midst of the chaos. Here are some ways to weave mindfulness into the fabric of your daily life:

1. Mindful Check-Ins: Pausing for Awareness

❖ **Short Breaks, Big Benefits:** Throughout your day, schedule brief mindful check-ins. These can be as short as 30 seconds and can be done anywhere, anytime.

❖ **Checking In With Yourself:** Close your eyes, take a few deep breaths, and gently turn your awareness inward. Notice your thoughts, emotions, and physical sensations without judgment.

❖ **Identifying Triggers:** Use these check-ins to identify potential triggers for stress or reactivity. Are you feeling overwhelmed, impatient, or frustrated? Recognizing these emotions early allows you to respond mindfully rather than reacting impulsively.

❖ **Mindful Micro-Practices:** Simple micro-practices like mindful breathing, short stretches, or a few seconds of progressive muscle relaxation can significantly reduce stress and refocus your attention.

2. Mindful Walking: Turning Errands into Opportunities

❖ **Walking with Presence:** We often underestimate the power of walking. Transform your everyday walks, whether it's a trip to the mailbox or a stroll with your child, into mindful experiences.

❖ **Engaging Your Senses:** Pay attention to the physical sensation of each step, the feel of the ground beneath your feet, and the rhythm of your breath.

❖ **Appreciating Your Surroundings:** Notice the sights and sounds around you. Observe the changing colors of the leaves, the chirping of birds, or the gentle breeze on your skin.

❖ **A Break from Technology:** Avoid distractions like phones or music during mindful walks. Allow yourself to be fully present in the moment and appreciate the simple beauty of your surroundings.

3. Mindful Parenting Moments: Connecting with Your Child

❖ **Putting Away Distractions:** When interacting with your child, put away your phone, silence notifications, and give them your full attention. Make eye contact and truly listen to what they have to say.

❖ **Active Listening:** Practice active listening skills. Reflect on what you hear, paraphrase their words to ensure understanding, and ask open-ended questions to encourage them to elaborate.

❖ **Empathic Responses:** Validate their emotions, even if you don't necessarily agree with them. Use phrases like "It sounds like you're feeling frustrated" or "I understand why you might be upset" to show empathy and create a safe space for expression.

❖ **Mindful Breathing:** If you feel yourself getting overwhelmed or frustrated, take a few deep breaths to center yourself before responding. This allows you to react mindfully rather than impulsively.

❖ **Transforming Challenging Moments:** Approach challenging situations with your child as opportunities for mindful co-parenting. Work together to problem-solve, brainstorm solutions, and find a resolution that works for everyone.

Integrating Mindfulness Throughout Your Day:

❖ **Schedule Reminders:** Set reminders on your phone or use sticky notes as prompts to take mindful check-ins throughout the day.

❖ **Find What Works for You:** Experiment with different mindful practices and discover what works best for you in different situations.

❖ **Be Patient with Yourself:** There will be times when you forget to be mindful. Don't beat yourself up; simply acknowledge it and gently bring your attention back to the present moment.

By incorporating these practices throughout your day, you'll cultivate a sense of calm and presence that allows you to navigate the inevitable ups and downs of parenthood with greater ease and grace. Remember, mindfulness is a skill that takes practice. Be patient with yourself, celebrate your progress, and enjoy the journey of weaving mindfulness into the fabric of your daily life.

Evening Routine

As the day winds down, creating a mindful evening routine allows you to transition from the busyness of the day to a state of peace and tranquility, promoting restful sleep. Here are key practices to integrate into your nighttime routine that will leave you feeling centered and prepared for a good night's sleep:

1. Digital Detox: Unplugging for Peace

❖ **Banishing Blue Light:** In the hour or so before bed, power down electronic devices like phones, laptops, and TVs. The blue light emitted from these screens disrupts the production of melatonin, a hormone essential for sleep regulation.

❖ **Alternative Activities:** Opt for calming activities that promote relaxation. Take a warm bath, curl up with a book (preferably a physical book to avoid screen glare), practice gentle yoga or stretching, or enjoy a cup of herbal tea.

❖ **Creating a Sleep Sanctuary:** Ensure your bedroom is a haven for sleep. Keep it quiet, dark, and cool. Consider using blackout curtains, earplugs, and keeping the room at a comfortable temperature.

2. Soothing the Mind and Body: Techniques for Relaxation

❖ **Mindful Breathing:** If you find your mind racing as you try to fall asleep, practice mindful breathing exercises. Focus on your breath, feeling the rise and fall of your chest with each inhalation and exhalation.

❖ **Progressive Muscle Relaxation:** This technique involves progressively tensing and relaxing different muscle groups throughout your body. As you release the tension, focus on the feeling of relaxation spreading through your body.

❖ **Guided Imagery:** Visualize calming scenes or experiences. Imagine yourself lying on a beach listening to the waves, or nestled in a cozy cabin by a crackling fireplace.

Consistency is key. By establishing a relaxing bedtime routine and incorporating these practices most nights of the week, you'll cultivate a sense of peace and tranquility that allows you to drift off to sleep with ease. As with all mindfulness practices, be patient with yourself. There will be nights when you struggle to unwind. Gently guide your attention back to your breath or your chosen relaxation technique, and trust that with practice, you'll establish an evening routine that promotes restorative sleep and sets the stage for a mindful and present tomorrow.

Mindful Transitions

Mindfulness isn't just about carving out dedicated chunks of time for meditation or reflection. It's about cultivating a state of present moment awareness throughout the tapestry of your daily life. Here are two practices you can integrate seamlessly into your day to create smoother transitions and minimize distractions:

1. Mindful Transitions: Rituals for Renewal

❖ **Marking the Moments:** Our days are filled with transitions – from work to home, errands to playtime with your child. These transitions can often feel jarring, leaving us feeling scattered and out of focus.

❖ **Creating Rituals:** Mindful transitions involve creating short, deliberate rituals to mark the end of one activity and the beginning of another. This allows you to mentally and emotionally shift gears and approach each task with renewed presence.

❖ **Examples of Rituals:** Take a few deep breaths before starting a new work project. Briefly stretch or shake out your body after a long car ride. Briefly close your eyes and set an intention for quality time with your children before you begin playing.

❖ **Benefits of Rituals:** These mindful transitions act as mini-cleanses, washing away the stress of the previous activity and allowing you to be fully present for the one at hand.

2. Mindful Technology Use: Finding Balance

❖ **Technology: A Double-Edged Sword:** Technology is an integral part of our lives, offering countless benefits. However, it can also be a significant source of distraction, hindering our ability to be mindful and present in the moment.

❖ **Setting Boundaries:** To cultivate mindfulness throughout your day, establish boundaries around technology use.

❖ **Examples of Boundaries:** Silence notifications during meals or playtime with your children. Designate specific times to check emails and social media, and avoid using them in bed.

❖ **Finding Balance:** The key is to find a balance. Technology can be a powerful tool, but it shouldn't control your attention. By setting boundaries, you reclaim control and create space for mindful presence in your daily life.

Mindfulness is a practice, not a destination. There will be times when you forget these practices or get pulled into distractions. Be patient with yourself, and gently bring your attention back to the present moment. By incorporating these practices throughout your day, you'll cultivate a sense of calm and focus that allows you to navigate the transitions and distractions of daily life with greater ease and grace.

Mindful Environment

Your environment has a profound impact on your well-being. By incorporating mindfulness into your surroundings, you can create a sanctuary that fosters peace, focus, and present-moment awareness. Here are two key practices to cultivate a mindful environment in your home, along with additional tips to amplify their impact:

1. Create Sacred Spaces: A Dedicated Corner for Calm

❖ **A Room Within a Room:** You don't need a dedicated meditation room to cultivate a mindful space. Even a small corner of your home can be transformed into a haven for relaxation and reflection.

❖ **Setting the Tone:** Use calming colors like light blues, greens, or lavenders. Opt for comfortable seating like a plush armchair or a meditation cushion. Minimize decorations, but consider incorporating elements that inspire you, such as a nature photograph, a calming piece of artwork, or a small indoor water feature.

❖ **A Multi-Purpose Retreat:** This dedicated space can be used for meditation practice, mindful breathing exercises, or simply a quiet place to retreat for a few moments of peace and reflection throughout the day. If space allows, consider adding a yoga mat or a small bookshelf with mindfulness resources.

❖ **Amplify the Effect:** Enhance the ambiance with aromatherapy. Diffuse calming essential oils like lavender, chamomile, or sandalwood. Play soft, nature-inspired music or guided meditations. Keep a mindfulness journal and pen in your designated space to capture thoughts and reflections.

2. Simplify Surroundings: Reducing Clutter for Clarity

❖ **Decluttering for Mindfulness:** Clutter can be a significant source of stress and distraction. A cluttered environment can make it difficult to focus and cultivate a sense of calm.

❖ **Letting Go:** Dedicate time to decluttering your living space, following the KonMari method or another decluttering philosophy that resonates with you. Discard unused items, organize belongings, and create a sense of order and simplicity.

❖ **Promoting Mental Clarity:** By simplifying your surroundings, you reduce visual clutter and create a space that promotes mental clarity and allows you to focus on the present moment.

❖ **Beyond Physical Clutter:** Mindful space extends beyond physical clutter. Consider the digital clutter that bombards you with notifications and information overload.

Schedule specific times to check emails and social media, and silence notifications during focused activities or relaxation time.

Creating a mindful environment is a journey, not a destination. It's not about achieving a picture-perfect space from a magazine. It's about creating a space that feels calming and supportive for you. Be patient with yourself, make gradual changes, and enjoy the process of transforming your home into a mindful sanctuary. As you cultivate this haven, you'll find it becomes a source of strength and rejuvenation, spilling over into all aspects of your life.

Mindful Self-Care

Parenting can be a demanding journey, filled with moments of joy and frustration in equal measure. Just as you tend to your child's needs, it's crucial to prioritize your own well-being. By incorporating mindful self-care practices into your routine, you cultivate resilience, compassion, and the inner strength to navigate the inevitable challenges of parenthood.

1. Self-Compassion Practices: Cultivating Kindness Within

❖ **The Power of Self-Acceptance:** We all make mistakes and experience moments of self-doubt. Mindfulness encourages self-compassion, allowing you to acknowledge these experiences with kindness and understanding rather than judgment.

❖ **Loving-Kindness Meditation:** This meditation practice involves sending yourself and others well wishes of love, peace, and happiness. Regular practice fosters self-compassion and a sense of inner peace. Consider using guided meditations or apps to support your practice.

❖ **Affirmations for Strength:** Positive affirmations can be powerful tools for self-compassion. Repeat mantras like "I am worthy" or "I am a good parent" to counter negative self-talk and cultivate self-belief. Post reminders around your house or write them on sticky notes to keep them top-of-mind.

❖ **Soothing Gestures:** During moments of stress or overwhelm, offer yourself physical gestures of comfort. Place a hand on your heart, take a few deep breaths, or gently rub your temples. These actions signal safety and self-care to your nervous system. Mindful self-touch can activate the relaxation response and help you regulate your emotions.

2. Nourishing Activities: Filling Your Cup

❖ **Beyond Just Checking Boxes:** Self-care isn't just about ticking things off a to-do list. It's about prioritizing activities that replenish your energy, nurture your spirit, and bring you joy.

❖ **Identifying Your Needs:** Take time to reflect on what truly nourishes you. Do you find solace in getting lost in a good book? Does spending time in nature restore your energy? Perhaps creative pursuits like painting or playing music bring you joy. Consider activities that engage your senses, allow you to express yourself creatively, or simply bring you a sense of peace and enjoyment.

❖ **Schedule Time for YOU:** Don't wait for a free moment to appear in your busy schedule. Block out time in your calendar, even if it's just 15 minutes a day, to engage in activities that nourish your mind, body, and soul. Treat these self-care appointments with the same respect you would a doctor's appointment or work meeting.

❖ **The Ripple Effect:** By filling your own cup with self-care, you become a more patient, present, and joyful parent. The benefits of prioritizing your well-being extend to your children and create a more positive and enriching environment for everyone. When you feel cared for and resourced, you're better equipped to respond to your child's needs with love and understanding, fostering a stronger parent-child bond.

Self-care is not selfish, it's essential. By integrating these practices into your daily routine, you cultivate a sense of self-compassion and prioritize activities that nourish you. As you become a more mindful and well-cared-for parent, you'll find yourself better equipped to navigate the joys and challenges of parenthood with greater ease and grace. Mindfulness is a practice, not a destination, so be patient with yourself. There will be days when self-care takes a backseat. The important thing is to recommit to your well-being and cultivate a sense of self-compassion throughout your parenting journey

Part 2: Cultivating Emotional Intelligence in Your Child

Chapter 4: The Emotional Landscape of Childhood

Development of Children's Emotions at Different Stages

Children's emotions undergo a remarkable journey of growth and transformation as they progress through various developmental stages. Understanding this emotional development is crucial for parents to provide appropriate support and guidance in nurturing their child's emotional intelligence.

The Early Years (Birth to 5)

The foundations of emotional development are laid during the earliest years of a child's life, and this period is marked by rapid growth and transformation in their emotional capacities. From birth, infants experience a range of basic emotions, such as contentment, distress, fear, and interest, which they express through physiological signals and behaviors like crying, cooing, and facial expressions.

Emotional Bonding and Attachment: The primary emotional need for infants is to develop a secure attachment with their caregivers. Responsive, nurturing care during this time helps infants learn to trust and feel safe, laying the groundwork for healthy emotional regulation and resilience.

When caregivers consistently respond to an infant's emotional cues with sensitivity and attunement, a strong emotional bond is formed. This secure attachment provides a secure base from which infants can confidently explore their environment and begin to develop emotional self-awareness and social skills.

Emotion Recognition and Expression: As language and cognitive abilities develop, toddlers (1-3 years) begin to recognize and label their own emotions, as well as the emotions of others. This is a period of intense emotional experiences, often characterized by tantrums, separation anxiety, and a heightened sensitivity to frustration and overstimulation.

During this stage, toddlers are learning to regulate their emotions through interactions with their caregivers. Consistent, patient, and empathetic responses from parents can help toddlers develop self-soothing strategies and a sense of emotional safety. Providing emotional coaching and validating their feelings can help toddlers learn to express emotions in healthy ways.

Emotional Complexity and Self-Awareness: In early childhood (3-5 years), children's emotional vocabulary and understanding continue to expand. They become more adept at recognizing and expressing complex emotions like jealousy, shame, and pride. Additionally, they begin to grasp the concept of multiple emotions occurring simultaneously, such as feeling both excited and scared about starting school.

This stage is crucial for developing emotional self-awareness and empathy. Through play, storytelling, and close relationships with caregivers and peers, children learn to identify and name their own emotions, as well as understand the emotional experiences of others. Encouraging emotional expression, teaching emotion regulation techniques, and modeling empathy are important during this stage.

Role of Parents and Caregivers: During the early years, it is essential for parents and caregivers to provide a nurturing and emotionally attuned environment that fosters emotional intelligence. This involves:

❖ Responding to emotional cues with sensitivity and empathy, building a secure attachment.

❖ Validating and naming children's emotions to promote emotional self-awareness.

❖ Teaching appropriate ways to express and regulate emotions through modeling and guidance.

❖ Creating opportunities for emotional exploration through play, storytelling, and open communication.

❖ Modeling healthy emotional expression and regulation in their own behavior.

❖ Establishing routines and structures that provide emotional security and predictability.

By laying a solid foundation of emotional awareness, regulation, and empathy during the early years, parents and caregivers can equip their children with the emotional intelligence skills they need to navigate future developmental stages with greater resilience and emotional well-being.

The Middle Years (6 to 12)

As children transition from the early years into the middle years, their emotional landscape undergoes significant shifts and complexities. During this period, their emotional development is heavily influenced by social dynamics, peer relationships, and academic pressures, marking a pivotal phase in cultivating emotional intelligence.

Self-Awareness and Self-Regulation: In the middle years, children become increasingly self-aware, able to recognize and label their own emotions with greater nuance. They develop a deeper understanding of the causes and consequences of their emotional experiences, as well as the ability to differentiate between various shades of emotions like frustration, anger, and rage.

At this stage, children also begin to refine their emotional regulation strategies, moving beyond the more basic techniques they learned in early childhood. They develop more advanced coping mechanisms, such as cognitive reappraisal (reframing situations in a more positive light), problem-solving skills, and the ability to delay gratification.

However, emotional regulation can still be a significant challenge during the middle years, as children navigate the heightened intensity of emotions that often accompanies the onset of puberty and hormonal changes.

Social and Interpersonal Skills: The middle years are a critical period for developing social and interpersonal emotional intelligence. Children become increasingly attuned to the emotions of their peers, and their ability to empathize and understand the perspectives of others grows substantially.

Navigating friendships, resolving conflicts, and developing a sense of self-worth and self-confidence become important emotional challenges during this period. Children learn to navigate the complexities of social emotions like embarrassment, guilt, pride, and envy, which can have a profound impact on their self-esteem and relationships.

Peer acceptance and belonging become increasingly important during the middle years, and children may experience intense emotions related to social dynamics, such as feeling left out, bullied, or judged by their peers.

Identity and Values: During the middle years, children also begin to explore and question their values, beliefs, and sense of purpose. This process of self-discovery can be emotionally turbulent, as children grapple with questions of identity, morality, and their place in the world.

They may experience complex emotions like existential anxiety, confusion, or a sense of disillusionment as they confront the realities of the world around them. This period is often marked by a heightened sensitivity to issues of fairness, justice, and social responsibility, which can evoke strong emotional responses.

Role of Parents and Caregivers: Providing a supportive and emotionally validating environment is crucial for helping children navigate the emotional complexities of the middle years. Parents and caregivers can play a vital role by:

❖ Encouraging open communication about emotions and creating a safe space for emotional expression.

❖ Teaching advanced emotion regulation strategies, such as cognitive reappraisal and mindfulness techniques.

❖ Modeling healthy emotional intelligence, including empathy, conflict resolution, and self-awareness.

❖ Providing guidance and support in navigating social dynamics and peer relationships.

❖ Fostering a sense of self-worth and promoting a growth mindset to build emotional resilience.

❖ Exploring values, beliefs, and identity in a non-judgmental and supportive manner.

By understanding the unique emotional challenges and developmental tasks of the middle years, parents and caregivers can better equip children with the emotional intelligence skills they need to thrive during this transitional phase and lay the groundwork for healthy emotional development in adolescence and beyond.

The Teenage Years (13 to 18+)

The transition into adolescence is marked by significant emotional upheaval and intensity, as teenagers navigate the complexities of physical, cognitive, and social changes. During this stage, emotional development is characterized by heightened sensitivity, volatility, and the quest for identity and independence.

Emotional Intensity and Hormonal Changes: One of the hallmarks of adolescence is the intense and rapidly fluctuating emotions that teenagers experience. Hormonal changes during puberty can contribute to mood swings, emotional reactivity, and a heightened sensitivity to stress and strong emotions like anger, sadness, and anxiety.

Teenagers may feel overwhelmed by the sheer intensity of their emotions, struggling to understand and regulate these powerful feelings. This emotional volatility can manifest in impulsive behavior, risk-taking, and conflicts with parents or authority figures.

Identity Formation and Self-Concept: The teenage years are a critical period for identity formation and the development of a coherent sense of self. Adolescents grapple with questions of "Who am I?" and "Where do I fit in?" as they explore different roles, values, and belief systems.

This process of self-discovery can evoke a range of emotions, including confusion, insecurity, pride, and a desire for autonomy and independence. Adolescents may experiment with different identities, affiliations, and behaviors, leading to potential conflicts with family or societal expectations.

Peer Relationships and Social Dynamics: Peer relationships and social dynamics play a significant role in emotional development during adolescence. Teenagers place a high value on peer acceptance and belonging, and their self-esteem and emotional well-being can be greatly influenced by their social experiences.

Navigating complex social dynamics, such as romantic relationships, cliques, and peer pressure, can evoke intense emotions like jealousy, insecurity, anxiety, and excitement. Adolescents may also struggle with issues of conformity versus individuality, as they strive to balance their need for acceptance with their desire for authenticity.

Existential Questioning and Meaning-Making: As cognitive abilities mature, adolescents often engage in existential questioning and meaning-making. They may grapple with deep questions about their purpose, values, and beliefs, leading to emotional experiences like disillusionment, uncertainty, or a sense of profound connection to larger issues.

This search for meaning can also involve exploring spirituality, philosophy, and social or political causes, which can evoke strong emotions and a desire for self-expression and social activism.

Role of Parents and Caregivers: Navigating the emotional complexities of adolescence can be challenging for both teenagers and their parents or caregivers. However, providing a supportive and emotionally validating environment is crucial during this stage:

- ❖ Foster open and non-judgmental communication about emotions and experiences.

- ❖ Encourage emotional expression and offer guidance on healthy emotion regulation strategies.

❖ Respect adolescents' need for autonomy and independence while maintaining appropriate boundaries.

❖ Model emotional intelligence, including self-awareness, empathy, and conflict resolution.

❖ Provide a safe and supportive environment for adolescents to explore their identity and values.

❖ Seek professional help if needed to address significant emotional distress or mental health concerns.

By understanding the unique emotional landscape of adolescence and providing a nurturing and supportive environment, parents and caregivers can help teenagers develop emotional intelligence, resilience, and a strong sense of self, preparing them for the challenges and opportunities that lie ahead in adulthood.

Throughout these developmental stages, it is crucial for parents to understand the unique emotional landscapes and needs of their children. By providing nurturing care, emotional validation, and guidance in developing emotional intelligence skills, parents can help their children navigate the complexities of emotional growth and foster resilience, self-awareness, and healthy emotional regulation.

Common Emotional Challenges Faced by Children

Tantrums:

Understanding and Addressing Emotional Outbursts in Children

Tantrums are a natural and common occurrence in the lives of many children, particularly toddlers and young children who are still developing their emotional regulation skills. These outbursts can be challenging for both children and caregivers, often leaving parents feeling overwhelmed and unsure of how to respond effectively. Understanding the underlying causes of tantrums and learning strategies to address them can help support children's emotional development and promote healthier coping mechanisms.

Understanding Tantrums: Tantrums are emotional outbursts characterized by intense displays of anger, frustration, or distress. They often involve behaviors such as screaming, crying, stomping, hitting, or throwing objects. While tantrums can be triggered by various factors, they typically occur when children feel overwhelmed by emotions and lack the ability to express themselves verbally or cope with their feelings effectively.

Causes of Tantrums: Several factors can contribute to the onset of tantrums in children:

❖ **Developmental Stage:** Tantrums are particularly common in toddlers and young children as they navigate the developmental milestones of emotional regulation and self-expression.

❖ **Communication Challenges**: Children may resort to tantrums when they struggle to communicate their needs, desires, or frustrations verbally. This is especially true for children who are still learning to speak or have limited language skills.

❖ **Overstimulation or Fatigue**: Overwhelming sensory input or fatigue from lack of sleep can increase a child's susceptibility to tantrums.

❖ **Frustration or Disappointment**: Children may become frustrated or upset when they encounter obstacles, experience disappointment, or are unable to have their needs met.

❖ **Changes in Routine or Environment**: Transitions, changes in routine, or unfamiliar environments can trigger anxiety and uncertainty in children, leading to tantrums as a coping mechanism.

Addressing Tantrums: While tantrums can be challenging to manage, there are several strategies parents and caregivers can employ to help children navigate their emotions and develop healthier coping mechanisms:

❖ **Stay Calm**: It's essential for adults to remain calm and composed when responding to tantrums. Taking deep breaths and maintaining a calm demeanor can help de-escalate the situation and model effective emotion regulation for the child.

❖ **Validate Emotions**: Acknowledge and validate the child's feelings, letting them know that it's okay to feel angry, frustrated, or upset. Empathize with their experience and reassure them that you're there to help.

❖ **Provide Verbal Support**: Encourage the child to use words to express their feelings and needs. Offer simple phrases or prompts to help them articulate what they're experiencing, such as "I see that you're feeling upset. Can you tell me what's wrong?"

❖ **Offer Distraction or Comfort**: Redirecting the child's attention to a different activity or providing a comforting hug can help soothe their emotions and shift their focus away from the trigger of the tantrum.

❖ **Set Limits and Boundaries**: While it's important to validate the child's emotions, it's also necessary to establish clear and consistent boundaries for behavior. Calmly communicate expectations and consequences, and follow through with gentle but firm guidance.

❖ **Teach Coping Strategies**: As children grow and develop, teach them age-appropriate coping strategies for managing their emotions, such as deep breathing, counting to ten, or taking a break in a quiet space.

❖ **Seek Support**: If tantrums persist or significantly interfere with the child's daily functioning, consider seeking guidance from a pediatrician, therapist, or child development specialist who can offer additional support and resources.

Reflections: Tantrums are a common and normal part of child development, often occurring when children feel overwhelmed, frustrated, or unable to communicate their needs effectively. By understanding the underlying causes of tantrums and employing strategies to address them, parents and caregivers can support children's emotional development, promote healthier coping mechanisms, and strengthen the parent-child relationship. With patience, empathy, and consistency, tantrums can become valuable opportunities for children to learn and grow in their emotional intelligence and self-regulation skills.

Anxiety:

Understanding and Supporting Children with Anxiety

Anxiety is a prevalent emotional challenge faced by many children, manifesting in various forms and impacting their daily lives in significant ways. Recognizing the signs of anxiety in children and providing appropriate support and guidance can help alleviate their distress and promote their emotional well-being.

Understanding Anxiety: Anxiety in children is a complex emotional state characterized by feelings of worry, fear, and apprehension. It can manifest in various forms, including separation anxiety, social anxiety, or generalized anxiety. Children experiencing anxiety may exhibit physical symptoms such as stomachaches, headaches, or difficulty sleeping. Understanding the nuances of anxiety in children is crucial for providing effective support and intervention.

Causes of Anxiety: Several factors can contribute to the development of anxiety in children:

❖ **Genetic Predisposition**: Children with a family history of anxiety disorders may be more likely to experience anxiety themselves due to genetic factors.

❖ **Environmental Stressors**: Stressful life events such as family conflicts, academic pressure, or changes in routine can trigger anxiety in children.

❖ **Traumatic Experiences**: Exposure to traumatic events such as accidents, natural disasters, or violence can lead to the development of anxiety in children.

❖ **Biological Factors**: Imbalances in neurotransmitters or hormonal fluctuations in the brain may contribute to the onset of anxiety disorders in children.

❖ **Cognitive Patterns**: Negative thought patterns, perfectionism, or excessive worry may exacerbate anxiety symptoms in children.

Addressing Anxiety: Supporting children with anxiety requires a multifaceted approach that addresses their emotional, cognitive, and behavioral needs:

❖ **Validation and Empathy**: Validate the child's feelings of anxiety and provide empathetic support. Let them know that it's normal to feel scared or worried and reassure them that you're there to help.

❖ **Teach Coping Strategies**: Teach the child coping strategies such as deep breathing, mindfulness, or progressive muscle relaxation to help them manage their anxiety symptoms.

❖ **Create a Safe Environment**: Foster a safe and supportive environment where the child feels comfortable expressing their feelings and seeking help when needed.

❖ **Establish Predictable Routines**: Establish consistent routines and clear expectations to reduce uncertainty and anxiety. Provide structure and predictability in the child's daily life.

❖ **Encourage Gradual Exposure**: Gradually expose the child to situations or activities that trigger their anxiety, helping them build resilience and confidence over time.

❖ **Seek Professional Help**: If a child's anxiety significantly interferes with their daily functioning or quality of life, seek guidance from a mental health professional who can provide specialized support and interventions.

Reflections: Anxiety is a common emotional challenge faced by many children, impacting their daily lives and emotional well-being. By understanding the causes of anxiety, addressing the underlying factors, and providing appropriate support and intervention, parents, caregivers, and educators can help children develop healthy coping mechanisms, build resilience, and thrive emotionally. With patience, empathy, and proactive intervention, children can learn to manage their anxiety effectively and lead fulfilling lives.

Frustration:

Understanding and Addressing Emotional Challenges in Children

Frustration is a common emotional response experienced by children when they encounter obstacles or challenges that impede their progress or success. It often arises when children struggle to master new skills, understand complex concepts, or express themselves effectively. Frustration can manifest as feelings of anger, impatience, disappointment, or helplessness.

Understanding Frustration: Frustration is a common emotional response experienced by children when they encounter obstacles or challenges that impede their progress or success. It often arises when children struggle to master new skills, understand complex concepts, or express themselves effectively. Frustration can manifest as feelings of anger, impatience, disappointment, or helplessness.

Causes of Frustration: Several factors can contribute to the experience of frustration in children:

❖ **Developmental Challenges**: Children may experience frustration as a natural part of their developmental process, particularly when learning new skills or adapting to changes in their environment.

❖ **Learning Difficulties**: Children with learning disabilities or cognitive challenges may face increased frustration when they encounter difficulties in academic or social settings.

❖ **High Expectations**: Unrealistic expectations from parents, teachers, or peers can exacerbate feelings of frustration in children, especially if they feel pressure to meet certain standards or performance goals.

❖ **Communication Barriers**: Difficulty expressing themselves verbally or understanding others can lead to frustration in children, particularly if they feel misunderstood or unable to convey their thoughts and feelings effectively.

❖ **Perceived Lack of Control**: Children may feel frustrated when they perceive a lack of control over their circumstances or outcomes, leading to feelings of powerlessness or inadequacy.

Addressing Frustration: Supporting children in managing their frustration requires a combination of empathy, patience, and practical strategies:

❖ **Validate Feelings**: Acknowledge and validate the child's feelings of frustration, letting them know that it's okay to feel upset or disappointed when faced with challenges.

❖ **Teach Problem-Solving Skills**: Help children develop problem-solving skills by breaking down tasks into smaller steps, brainstorming possible solutions, and encouraging experimentation and persistence.

❖ **Provide Support and Encouragement**: Offer support and encouragement to children as they navigate challenges, emphasizing effort and progress rather than focusing solely on outcomes.

❖ **Model Positive Coping Strategies**: Demonstrate healthy ways of coping with frustration, such as taking deep breaths, seeking help from others, or taking a break and returning to the task later.

❖ **Encourage Growth Mindset**: Foster a growth mindset in children by emphasizing the importance of effort, resilience, and learning from mistakes. Encourage them to view setbacks as opportunities for growth and learning rather than failures.

❖ **Create a Positive Learning Environment**: Establish a positive and supportive learning environment where children feel safe to take risks, make mistakes, and ask for help without fear of judgment or criticism.

Reflections: Frustration is a natural and common emotional response experienced by children when they encounter obstacles or challenges in their lives. By understanding the causes of frustration and implementing strategies to address it effectively, parents, caregivers, and educators can help children develop resilience, problem-solving skills, and a positive mindset that will serve them well throughout their lives. With patience, empathy, and support, children can learn to navigate challenges and setbacks with confidence and perseverance.

Anger:

Understanding and Addressing Emotional Outbursts in Children

Like adults, children experience anger as a natural response to perceived threats, injustices, or frustrations. Anger can range from mild irritation to intense outbursts and may be triggered by various factors, including feeling misunderstood, excluded, or unfairly treated.

Understanding Anger: Anger is a complex emotion characterized by feelings of displeasure, irritation, or hostility. In children, anger can manifest in different ways, such as verbal outbursts, physical aggression, or withdrawal. While anger itself is not inherently negative, how children express and manage their anger can significantly impact their well-being and relationships.

Causes of Anger: Several factors can contribute to the experience of anger in children:

❖ **Frustration:** Children may become angry when they encounter obstacles or challenges that thwart their goals or desires, leading to feelings of frustration and powerlessness.

❖ **Feeling Misunderstood or Invalidated**: Children may feel angry when they perceive that their thoughts, feelings, or experiences are not understood or taken seriously by others.

❖ **Unmet Needs or Expectations**: Anger can arise when children's needs or expectations are not met, whether its attention, approval, autonomy, or material desires.

❖ **External Stressors**: Stressful events or changes in the child's environment, such as family conflicts, academic pressures, or transitions, can trigger feelings of anger and agitation.

❖ **Modeling Behavior**: Children may learn to express anger from observing the behavior of adults or peers in their environment, particularly if anger is used as a primary means of communication or problem-solving.

Addressing Anger: Supporting children in managing their anger requires a comprehensive approach that addresses both the underlying causes and the expression of anger itself:

❖ **Teach Emotional Awareness**: Help children recognize and label their emotions, including anger, and understand the physiological signs and triggers associated with anger.

❖ **Encourage Healthy Expression**: Provide opportunities for children to express their anger in constructive ways, such as through art, writing, or physical activity. Encourage them to use "I" statements to express their feelings and needs assertively.

❖ **Practice Self-Regulation Skills**: Teach children strategies for managing their anger and calming themselves down when feeling upset, such as deep breathing, mindfulness, or progressive muscle relaxation.

❖ **Model Positive Coping**: Model healthy ways of dealing with anger and conflict resolution in your own behavior, demonstrating empathy, active listening, and assertive communication.

❖ **Set Clear Expectations and Boundaries**: Establish clear expectations for behavior and consequences for inappropriate expression of anger. Encourage children to take responsibility for their actions and make amends when necessary.

❖ **Provide Support and Validation**: Validate children's feelings of anger and provide a supportive environment where they feel safe to express themselves without fear of judgment or punishment.

❖ **Seek Professional Help if Needed**: If a child's anger significantly interferes with their daily functioning or relationships, consider seeking guidance from a mental health professional who can provide specialized support and interventions.

Anger is a natural and common emotion experienced by children, often in response to perceived threats, injustices, or frustrations. By understanding the underlying causes of anger and providing appropriate support and guidance, parents, caregivers, and educators can help children develop healthy coping mechanisms, emotional regulation skills, and constructive ways of expressing and managing their anger. With patience, empathy, and proactive intervention, children can learn to navigate their emotions effectively and build positive relationships with others.

Sadness:

Understanding and Addressing Emotional Challenges in Children

Children, like adults, experience sadness as a natural emotional response to various life events and circumstances. Sadness can manifest in children in response to loss, disappointment, or changes in their lives, and it's essential for caregivers to understand and address these emotions effectively.

Understanding Sadness: Sadness is a complex emotion characterized by feelings of unhappiness, grief, or melancholy. In children, sadness can manifest in different ways, such as tearfulness, withdrawal, irritability, or changes in behavior. While sadness is a normal and healthy emotion, prolonged or intense feelings of sadness can impact a child's well-being and functioning.

Causes of Sadness: Several factors can contribute to the experience of sadness in children:

❖ **Loss or Grief**: Children may experience sadness in response to the loss of a loved one, pet, or significant relationship. Grief can also arise from changes in family structure, such as divorce, separation, or relocation.

❖ **Disappointment or Rejection**: Children may feel sad when their expectations are not met, whether it's receiving a negative outcome, not achieving a desired goal, or experiencing rejection or exclusion from peers.

❖ **Transitions or Changes**: Sadness can arise from transitions or changes in a child's life, such as starting a new school, moving to a new neighborhood, or experiencing significant life events like the birth of a sibling.

❖ **Bullying or Peer Conflict**: Children may experience sadness in response to peer conflict, bullying, or social rejection. Feeling misunderstood or excluded by peers can contribute to feelings of sadness and loneliness.

❖ **Internal Struggles**: Children may also experience sadness as a result of internal struggles, such as low self-esteem, perfectionism, or feelings of inadequacy.

Addressing Sadness: Supporting children in managing their sadness requires empathy, validation, and practical strategies for coping:

❖ **Provide Emotional Support**: Offer comfort, reassurance, and a listening ear to children when they express sadness. Let them know that it's okay to feel sad and that you're there to support them through difficult emotions.

❖ **Encourage Expression**: Encourage children to express their feelings through art, writing, or storytelling. Provide opportunities for them to talk about what's bothering them and express their emotions in a safe and supportive environment.

❖ **Validate Feelings**: Validate children's feelings of sadness and let them know that their emotions are normal and valid. Avoid minimizing or dismissing their feelings, and instead, acknowledge their experience with empathy and understanding.

❖ **Teach Coping Skills**: Teach children healthy coping skills for managing sadness, such as deep breathing, relaxation techniques, or engaging in activities they enjoy. Encourage them to seek out positive distractions and engage in self-care activities that promote emotional well-being.

❖ **Promote Social Connections**: Help children foster supportive relationships with peers, family members, or trusted adults who can offer companionship, empathy, and understanding during times of sadness.

❖ **Seek Professional Help if Needed**: If a child's sadness persists or significantly interferes with their daily functioning or well-being, consider seeking guidance from a mental health professional who can provide specialized support and interventions tailored to their needs.

Reflections: Sadness is a natural and common emotion experienced by children in response to various life events and circumstances. By understanding the underlying causes of sadness and providing appropriate support and guidance, parents, caregivers, and educators can help children navigate their emotions effectively and develop healthy coping mechanisms. With patience, empathy, and proactive intervention, children can learn to manage their sadness in constructive ways and build resilience in the face of life's challenges.

Low Self-Esteem:

Understanding and Supporting Children's Emotional Well-Being

Children may struggle with feelings of inadequacy or low self-worth, particularly if they face criticism, comparison with peers, or challenges in achieving their goals. Low self-esteem can impact various aspects of a child's life, including academic performance, social relationships, and emotional well-being. It's crucial for caregivers to understand the signs and causes of low self-esteem in children and provide support to help them develop a positive sense of self.

Understanding Low Self-Esteem: Low self-esteem refers to a negative perception of oneself and one's abilities. Children with low self-esteem may doubt their worth, abilities, or value, leading to feelings of insecurity, inferiority, or self-doubt. Low self-esteem can manifest in behaviors such as social withdrawal, avoidance of challenges, self-criticism, or seeking validation from others.

Causes of Low Self-Esteem: Several factors can contribute to the development of low self-esteem in children:

❖ **Negative Feedback:** Harsh criticism, ridicule, or rejection from parents, peers, or authority figures can undermine a child's confidence and self-worth.

❖ **Social Comparison:** Constant comparison with peers or unrealistic societal standards can lead to feelings of inadequacy and inferiority in children.

❖ **Academic Challenges:** Difficulty in school, academic failure, or negative feedback from teachers can impact a child's perception of their academic abilities and intelligence.

❖ **Family Environment:** Family dynamics, parenting styles, and experiences of neglect, abuse, or dysfunction can influence a child's self-esteem and sense of worth.

❖ **Traumatic Experiences**: Traumatic events such as bullying, loss, or significant life changes can erode a child's confidence and self-esteem over time.

Supporting Children with Low Self-Esteem: Caregivers play a critical role in supporting children with low self-esteem and helping them develop a positive sense of self:

❖ **Promote Positive Self-Talk**: Encourage children to practice positive self-talk and challenge negative beliefs about themselves. Teach them to replace self-critical thoughts with affirmations and statements of self-acceptance and self-compassion.

❖ **Celebrate Effort and Progress**: Focus on effort rather than outcome and celebrate children's achievements, no matter how small. Acknowledge their strengths, talents, and unique qualities to boost their self-confidence and self-worth.

❖ **Provide Unconditional Love and Acceptance**: Offer unconditional love, acceptance, and support to children, regardless of their achievements or behavior. Show them that they are valued and loved for who they are, not just for what they do.

❖ **Encourage Independence and Autonomy**: Foster independence and autonomy in children by allowing them to make choices, solve problems, and take on responsibilities. Encourage them to explore their interests and pursue activities that bring them joy and fulfillment.

❖ **Create a Supportive Environment**: Create a supportive and nurturing environment where children feel safe to express themselves, take risks, and make mistakes without fear of judgment or criticism.

❖ **Seek Professional Help if Needed**: If low self-esteem significantly impacts a child's well-being or functioning, consider seeking guidance from a mental health professional who can provide specialized support and interventions tailored to their needs.

Reflections: Low self-esteem can significantly impact a child's emotional well-being, academic performance, and social relationships. By understanding the causes of low self-esteem and providing support and validation, caregivers can help children develop a positive sense of self, resilience, and confidence in their abilities. With patience, empathy, and consistent support, children can learn to overcome feelings of inadequacy and cultivate a healthy sense of self-esteem that will serve them well throughout their lives.

Loneliness:

Understanding and Addressing Children's Emotional Well-Being

Children may experience feelings of loneliness and isolation, especially if they have difficulty making friends, feel disconnected from their peers, or experience changes in their social environment. Loneliness can have a significant impact on a child's mental and emotional health, affecting their self-esteem, academic performance, and overall well-being. It's essential for caregivers to recognize the signs of loneliness in children and provide support to help them build meaningful connections and friendships.

Understanding Loneliness: Loneliness refers to a subjective feeling of social isolation or disconnectedness, even when surrounded by others.

Children who experience loneliness may feel misunderstood, excluded, or lacking in meaningful relationships. Loneliness can manifest in various ways, including withdrawal from social activities, reluctance to engage with peers, or seeking attention and validation from others.

Causes of Loneliness: Several factors can contribute to feelings of loneliness in children:

❖ **Difficulty Making Friends**: Children who struggle with social skills, shyness, or anxiety may find it challenging to initiate and maintain friendships, leading to feelings of loneliness and social isolation.

❖ **Changes in Social Environment**: Transitions such as moving to a new school, neighborhood, or community can disrupt established social connections and leave children feeling disconnected from their peers.

❖ **Bullying or Peer Rejection**: Experiences of bullying, exclusion, or rejection from peers can contribute to feelings of loneliness and alienation in children, eroding their sense of belonging and self-worth.

❖ **Family Dynamics**: Family dynamics, such as parental divorce, neglect, or parental absence, can impact a child's sense of security and connectedness, leading to feelings of loneliness and emotional distress.

❖ **Cultural or Language Barriers**: Children who are part of minority groups or who speak a different language may experience difficulties in forming connections with peers due to cultural or language barriers, increasing feelings of loneliness and social isolation.

Supporting Children with Loneliness: Caregivers play a crucial role in supporting children with loneliness and helping them develop meaningful connections and relationships:

❖ **Encourage Social Engagement:** Encourage children to participate in social activities, clubs, or sports where they can meet and interact with peers who share similar interests and hobbies.

❖ **Facilitate Friendships:** Help children develop social skills and navigate social situations by role-playing, providing guidance on initiating conversations, and encouraging empathy and inclusivity.

❖ **Foster Connection at Home:** Create opportunities for meaningful connection and bonding within the family by spending quality time together, engaging in shared activities, and fostering open communication and emotional support.

❖ **Promote Peer Acceptance:** Encourage empathy, kindness, and acceptance among peers by modeling inclusive behavior, addressing bullying or exclusion, and fostering a culture of belonging and respect in social settings.

❖ **Seek Professional Support if Needed:** If loneliness significantly impacts a child's well-being or functioning, consider seeking guidance from a mental health professional who can provide specialized support and interventions tailored to their needs.

Reflections: Loneliness can have a profound impact on a child's mental and emotional well-being, affecting their self-esteem, social relationships, and overall quality of life. By understanding the causes of loneliness and providing support to help children build meaningful connections and friendships, caregivers can help alleviate feelings of isolation and promote positive social development. With patience, empathy, and consistent support, children can develop the social skills and resilience needed to navigate social interactions and form lasting, meaningful relationships that contribute to their happiness and well-being.

Grief:

Navigating Children's Emotional Responses to Loss and Change

Children may experience grief in response to various life events, such as the loss of a loved one, a pet, or a significant life change like moving to a new home or school. Grief is a complex and multifaceted emotion that can evoke a range of feelings, including sadness, anger, confusion, and longing. It's essential for caregivers to understand the dynamics of grief in children and provide support to help them navigate their emotions during times of loss and transition.

Understanding Grief: Grief is a natural response to loss, encompassing emotional, psychological, and physical reactions to the absence of someone or something significant in a person's life. Children may experience grief in various contexts, including:

❖ **Loss of a Loved One:** The death of a family member, friend, or caregiver can profoundly impact a child's sense of security and well-being, leading to feelings of sadness, emptiness, and loss.

❖ **Loss of a Pet:** Pets play a significant role in children's lives, and the death or loss of a beloved pet can trigger feelings of grief and mourning similar to those experienced with human loss.

❖ **Life Changes**: Significant life changes such as parental divorce, relocation, or separation from friends can also evoke feelings of grief and loss in children as they adjust to new circumstances and navigate the transition.

Causes of Grief: Understanding Loss and Transition

Grief can be triggered by various life events and circumstances that result in a sense of loss or change. Understanding the underlying causes of grief can provide insight into the emotional experiences children may face and help caregivers provide appropriate support and guidance. Some common causes of grief in children include:

❖ **Death of a Loved One**: The death of a family member, friend, or caregiver is one of the most significant and profound causes of grief in children. Whether it's the loss of a parent, grandparent, sibling, or close friend, the absence of someone significant in a child's life can evoke intense feelings of sadness, confusion, and longing.

❖ **Loss of a Pet**: Pets play an important role in children's lives, often serving as companions, playmates, and sources of comfort and affection. The death or loss of a beloved pet can be deeply distressing for children, triggering feelings of grief and mourning similar to those experienced with human loss.

❖ **Divorce or Separation**: Family changes such as parental divorce, separation, or the loss of a caregiver can disrupt children's sense of security and stability, leading to feelings of grief and loss. Children may mourn the loss of the family unit, changes in living arrangements, and the absence of a parent or primary caregiver.

❖ **Relocation or Change in Schools**: Moving to a new home or school can be a significant source of grief and loss for children, especially if it involves leaving behind familiar surroundings, friends, and routines. Adjusting to a new environment and navigating changes in social relationships can evoke feelings of sadness, loneliness, and uncertainty.

❖ **Loss of Relationships or Friendships**: The loss of friendships, social rejection, or changes in peer relationships can be painful and challenging for children, particularly during times of transition such as starting school or moving to a new community. Feelings of rejection, isolation, and loneliness may contribute to grief and emotional distress.

❖ **Traumatic Experiences**: Children may experience grief in response to traumatic events such as accidents, natural disasters, or witnessing violence or harm. These experiences can shatter a child's sense of safety and security, leading to feelings of fear, confusion, and grief as they process the event and its impact on their lives.

❖ **Miscarriage or Loss of a Sibling**: Pregnancy loss, miscarriage, or the death of a sibling can be profoundly distressing for children and families, triggering feelings of grief, sadness, and confusion. Children may struggle to understand the loss and its implications for their family dynamics and future.

Manifestations of Grief: Grief can manifest differently in children depending on their age, developmental stage, and individual temperament:

❖ **Young Children**: Young children may struggle to understand the concept of death and may exhibit behaviors such as confusion, regressive behavior, clinginess, or asking repetitive questions about the deceased.

❖ **School-Age Children**: School-age children may experience a wide range of emotions, including sadness, anger, guilt, and fear. They may also express their grief through changes in behavior, academic performance, or social interactions.

❖ **Adolescents**: Adolescents may grapple with intense and conflicting emotions, including anger, resentment, and a sense of injustice. They may also withdraw from social activities, engage in risky behaviors, or experience disruptions in their relationships with peers and family members.

Supporting Children in Grief: Caregivers can play a vital role in supporting children through the grieving process and helping them cope with loss and change:

❖ **Provide Emotional Support**: Offer comfort, empathy, and a listening ear to children as they navigate their emotions. Validate their feelings and let them know that it's okay to grieve in their own way and at their own pace.

❖ **Encourage Expression**: Create opportunities for children to express their feelings through art, writing, storytelling, or play. Encourage open communication and provide space for them to share memories, thoughts, and emotions related to the loss.

❖ **Maintain Routines and Structure**: Maintain a sense of stability and predictability in children's lives by preserving familiar routines, rituals, and activities. Structure can provide a sense of security and comfort during times of uncertainty and upheaval.

❖ **Offer Age-Appropriate Information**: Provide children with honest and age-appropriate information about death, loss, and grief. Answer their questions truthfully and reassure them that their feelings are normal and natural.

❖ **Seek Professional Support if Needed**: If a child's grief significantly impacts their daily functioning or well-being, consider seeking guidance from a mental health professional who can provide specialized support and interventions tailored to their needs.

Reflections: Grief is a natural and universal response to loss and change, affecting children's emotional, psychological, and social well-being. By understanding the dynamics of grief in children and providing compassionate support and guidance, caregivers can help children navigate their emotions and develop resilience in the face of loss and transition. With patience, empathy, and consistent support, children can learn to process their grief in healthy ways and find meaning and healing in their experiences of loss and change.

Emphasizing the Importance of Emotional Validation

Emotional validation is a fundamental aspect of supporting children through grief and helping them navigate their emotions in healthy and constructive ways. By acknowledging and validating children's feelings, caregivers can create a safe and supportive environment where children feel understood, accepted, and supported in their grieving process. Here are several reasons why emotional validation is essential:

Affirms Children's Experiences:

Emotional validation plays a crucial role in affirming children's experiences by acknowledging the validity and significance of their feelings. When caregivers validate children's emotions, they reassure them that their emotional responses are normal and natural reactions to the challenges and transitions they are facing. By affirming children's experiences, emotional validation helps to normalize their emotions, reduce feelings of shame, guilt, or confusion, and foster a sense of acceptance and understanding.

Validation of Normalcy: Children often experience a wide range of emotions in response to loss and change, including sadness, anger, fear, and confusion. These emotions may be unfamiliar or overwhelming for children, leading them to question the validity of their feelings or worry that there is something wrong with them. Emotional validation reassures children that their emotions are entirely normal and understandable given their circumstances. By affirming the normalcy of their feelings, caregivers help children recognize that their emotional responses are valid and acceptable, validating their experiences and emotions as legitimate and understandable.

Normalization of Emotions: Loss and change can evoke powerful and sometimes overwhelming emotions in children, leading them to feel isolated or different from their peers. Emotional validation helps to normalize these emotions by acknowledging that they are common and expected responses to challenging situations. When caregivers validate children's experiences, they communicate that it is okay to feel sad, angry, or afraid in response to loss and change. By normalizing their emotions, emotional validation reduces feelings of isolation and alienation, reassuring children that they are not alone in their experiences and providing them with a sense of belonging and acceptance.

Reduction of Negative Self-Perceptions: Children may internalize negative beliefs about themselves or their emotions when they perceive their feelings as abnormal or unacceptable. Emotional validation helps to counteract these negative self-perceptions by affirming the validity and significance of children's emotions. When caregivers validate children's experiences, they communicate that it is okay to feel the way they do and that their emotions are worthy of acknowledgment and respect. By reducing feelings of shame, guilt, or confusion, emotional validation promotes positive self-esteem and self-acceptance, empowering children to embrace and express their emotions authentically and without judgment.

Fostering Open Communication: Emotional validation creates a supportive and nurturing environment where children feel comfortable expressing their thoughts, feelings, and concerns openly and honestly. When caregivers validate children's experiences, they encourage open communication and dialogue, fostering a sense of trust and connection in the parent-child relationship. By affirming the validity and significance of children's feelings, emotional validation creates a safe space for children to share their emotions without fear of judgment or rejection, strengthening the bond between caregivers and children and promoting healthy emotional development.

Promotes Emotional Expression:

Emotional expression is a vital aspect of children's emotional development, enabling them to communicate their feelings, thoughts, and concerns effectively. When children feel validated, they are more inclined to express themselves openly and honestly, leading to meaningful interactions and fostering a deeper connection between caregivers and children. Emotional validation plays a key role in promoting emotional expression by creating a supportive and nurturing environment where children feel safe to share their innermost thoughts and feelings without fear of judgment or rejection.

Encourages Authenticity: Emotional validation encourages children to embrace their authentic selves and express their emotions genuinely. When caregivers validate children's feelings, they communicate that it is okay to experience a wide range of emotions and that all feelings are valid and worthy of acknowledgment. This validation empowers children to express themselves authentically, without fear of criticism or invalidation, fostering a sense of self-acceptance and confidence in their emotional experiences.

Fosters Open Dialogue: Emotional validation fosters open dialogue and communication between caregivers and children, creating opportunities for meaningful interactions and connections. When caregivers validate children's emotions, they create a safe space for children to share their thoughts, feelings, and concerns openly and honestly. This open dialogue encourages children to communicate their emotions in a healthy and constructive manner, strengthening the bond between caregivers and children and promoting trust and understanding in the parent-child relationship.

Supports Emotional Regulation: Encouraging emotional expression through validation helps children develop healthy emotional regulation skills. When children feel validated, they learn to recognize, identify, and express their emotions in a constructive way, rather than suppressing or denying them. This promotes emotional resilience and adaptive coping strategies, enabling children to navigate challenging situations and regulate their emotions effectively.

Enhances Social and Emotional Skills: Emotional expression is essential for building social and emotional skills, such as empathy, communication, and conflict resolution. When children learn to express their emotions openly and honestly, they develop a better understanding of their own feelings and the feelings of others. This enhances their ability to communicate effectively, resolve conflicts peacefully, and build positive relationships with peers and caregivers.

Encourages Problem-Solving: Emotional expression through validation encourages children to seek support and guidance from caregivers when faced with challenges or difficult emotions. By expressing their feelings openly, children can work collaboratively with caregivers to identify solutions, cope with stressors, and navigate obstacles effectively. This fosters a sense of empowerment and self-efficacy in children, enabling them to develop problem-solving skills and resilience in the face of adversity.

Builds Trust and Connection:

Validation of children's emotions is a cornerstone of building trust and nurturing a strong bond between caregivers and children. When caregivers validate children's feelings, they demonstrate empathy, understanding, and respect, creating a safe and supportive environment where children feel valued and accepted. This validation fosters trust and strengthens the parent-child relationship in several ways:

1. Demonstrates Empathy and Understanding: Validating children's emotions shows that caregivers are attuned to their feelings and empathetic towards their experiences. When caregivers acknowledge and validate children's emotions, they communicate that they understand and accept their perspective, fostering a sense of empathy and connection in the parent-child relationship.

2. Creates a Safe and Supportive Environment: Emotional validation creates a safe space where children feel comfortable expressing their thoughts, feelings, and concerns without fear of judgment or rejection. When caregivers validate children's emotions, they reassure them that it's okay to experience a wide range of feelings and that their emotions will be acknowledged and respected. This safe and supportive environment builds trust and encourages open communication between caregivers and children.

3. Deepens Sense of Connection: Validating children's emotions deepens the sense of connection and intimacy in the parent-child relationship. When caregivers validate children's feelings, children feel heard, seen, and understood, strengthening their bond with caregivers and enhancing their sense of security and belonging. This deep connection forms the foundation of a positive and nurturing relationship built on trust, empathy, and mutual respect.

4. Encourages Authenticity and Vulnerability: Emotional validation encourages children to be authentic and vulnerable in expressing their emotions. When caregivers validate children's feelings, they create a space where children feel safe to be themselves and share their innermost thoughts and feelings openly and honestly. This authenticity fosters a deeper sense of connection and intimacy, allowing caregivers and children to build a relationship based on honesty and trust.

5. Promotes Emotional Regulation and Coping: A trusting and connected relationship with caregivers provides children with a sense of security and stability, which is essential for emotional regulation and coping. When children feel validated and supported by caregivers, they are better equipped to manage their emotions, cope with stressors, and navigate challenges effectively. This promotes resilience and fosters healthy emotional development in children.

Enhances Emotional Regulation:

Validating children's emotions plays a significant role in enhancing their emotional regulation skills, which are essential for navigating the complexities of emotions effectively. Emotional validation teaches children to identify, express, and manage their feelings in constructive ways, promoting resilience and adaptive coping strategies. Here's how validating children's emotions enhances their emotional regulation:

1. Recognizing and Identifying Emotions: When caregivers validate children's emotions, they help them recognize and identify their feelings accurately. By acknowledging and naming their emotions, children gain a deeper understanding of their inner experiences, allowing them to distinguish between different emotions and their underlying triggers. This awareness is foundational for emotional regulation, as children learn to recognize their emotional states and respond appropriately.

2. Expressing Emotions Openly: Emotional validation creates a safe space for children to express their emotions openly and honestly. When children feel validated, they are more likely to communicate their feelings instead of suppressing or denying them. By encouraging emotional expression, caregivers help children release pent-up emotions and reduce emotional arousal, promoting emotional regulation and preventing emotional dysregulation.

3. Managing Intense Emotions: Validating children's emotions teaches them healthy coping strategies for managing intense emotions effectively. When children feel validated, they learn that it's okay to experience strong emotions and that they have the support and resources to cope with them. Caregivers can teach children relaxation techniques, mindfulness practices, and problem-solving skills to regulate their emotions and reduce emotional distress.

4. Building Resilience and Coping Skills: Emotional validation fosters resilience by empowering children to cope with adversity and bounce back from challenges. When children feel validated, they develop confidence in their ability to navigate difficult emotions and situations, leading to increased resilience and emotional strength. By providing a supportive and nurturing environment, caregivers help children build coping skills and develop adaptive strategies for managing stressors and setbacks.

5. Promoting Adaptive Coping Mechanisms: When children feel validated, they are better equipped to cope with grief, loss, and other life transitions in adaptive ways. Emotional validation encourages children to express their feelings and seek support from caregivers and peers, rather than resorting to maladaptive coping mechanisms such as avoidance or withdrawal. By promoting adaptive coping strategies, caregivers help children navigate the ups and downs of life with resilience and grace.

Encourages Coping and Resilience:

Emotional validation plays a crucial role in empowering children to develop coping strategies and resilience when facing loss and adversity. By validating children's emotions, caregivers provide a supportive foundation for children to explore their feelings, process their grief, and find meaning and healing in their experiences. Here's how emotional validation encourages coping and resilience:

1. Providing Supportive Foundation: Emotional validation creates a safe and supportive environment where children feel comfortable expressing their emotions and seeking support from caregivers. When children feel validated, they know that their feelings are acknowledged and accepted, fostering a sense of security and trust. This supportive foundation serves as a buffer against the challenges of grief and loss, empowering children to cope with their emotions effectively.

2. Exploring and Processing Feelings: When caregivers validate children's emotions, they encourage them to explore and process their feelings in a healthy and constructive manner. Children are given the space and permission to express their emotions openly, without fear of judgment or rejection. This allows children to gain insight into their feelings, understand the underlying causes of their grief, and begin the process of healing and recovery.

3. Finding Meaning and Healing: Emotional validation helps children find meaning and healing in their experiences of grief and loss. When caregivers validate children's emotions, they validate the significance of their experiences and help them make sense of their feelings. Children are encouraged to reflect on their experiences, identify sources of support and strength, and find meaning in their journey of healing. This sense of purpose and understanding promotes resilience and facilitates the healing process.

4. Building Coping Strategies: Emotional validation empowers children to develop coping strategies and adaptive mechanisms for managing grief and loss. When children feel validated, they learn to recognize their emotional needs and seek out healthy coping strategies such as talking to supportive individuals, engaging in creative outlets, or practicing self-care activities. Caregivers can provide guidance and support as children explore different coping strategies, helping them build resilience and navigate the challenges of grief with grace.

5. Strengthening Resilience: By validating children's emotions, caregivers foster resilience and emotional strength in children. When children feel supported and validated in their experiences of grief and loss, they learn to adapt to adversity, bounce back from setbacks, and grow stronger in the process. Emotional validation teaches children that it's okay to experience difficult emotions and that they have the inner resources and support network to overcome challenges and thrive.

Practical Strategies for Emotional Validation:

Active Listening:

Active listening is a foundational strategy for emotional validation, allowing caregivers to demonstrate empathy, understanding, and support for children's emotions. Here are practical steps for implementing active listening to validate children's feelings effectively:

1. Create a Safe and Welcoming Environment: Ensure that the environment is conducive to open and honest communication, free from distractions and interruptions. Choose a quiet and comfortable space where children feel safe and comfortable sharing their thoughts and feelings.

2. Give Your Full Attention: Demonstrate your commitment to listening by giving your full attention to the child. Maintain eye contact, adopt an open body posture, and focus on the child's words and nonverbal cues. Show genuine interest in what the child has to say.

3. Listen Without Judgment: Practice nonjudgmental listening, suspending your own opinions, assumptions, and biases. Avoid interrupting or dismissing the child's feelings, even if they differ from your own perspective. Create a judgment-free space where children feel accepted and valued for their emotions.

4. Reflect and Validate Emotions: Reflect back the child's emotions and experiences to validate their feelings. Use empathetic statements to acknowledge the child's perspective and show that you understand and accept their emotions. For example, you might say, "It sounds like you're feeling really frustrated right now," or "I can see that you're feeling sad about what happened."

5. Validate the Child's Perspective: Acknowledge the validity of the child's perspective, even if you don't necessarily agree with it. Respect the child's feelings and experiences as valid and worthy of consideration. Avoid minimizing or invalidating the child's emotions, as this can undermine their sense of self-worth and confidence in expressing their feelings.

6. Ask Open-Ended Questions: Encourage further exploration and expression of emotions by asking open-ended questions. Invite the child to share more about their feelings, thoughts, and experiences without imposing your own interpretations or assumptions. Use prompts such as, "Can you tell me more about how you're feeling?" or "What do you think caused you to feel this way?"

7. Validate Nonverbal Cues: Pay attention to the child's nonverbal cues, such as body language, facial expressions, and tone of voice. Validate these cues by acknowledging the emotions they convey. For example, you might say, "I noticed that you're frowning. Are you feeling upset about something?"

8. Offer Support and Validation: Provide reassurance and validation throughout the conversation, emphasizing that it's normal and healthy to experience a range of emotions. Offer words of encouragement and support, affirming the child's resilience and strength in expressing their feelings. Let the child know that you are there to support them and help them navigate their emotions.

Empathetic Responses:

Empathetic responses are essential for validating children's emotions and demonstrating compassion and understanding. By responding to children's emotions with empathy, caregivers acknowledge the significance of their feelings and provide the support and validation they need to navigate their emotions effectively. Here are practical tips for offering empathetic responses to children's emotions:

1. Acknowledge the Child's Feelings: Begin by acknowledging the child's emotions with empathy and compassion. Use empathetic statements to reflect the child's feelings and show that you understand and accept their emotional experience. For example, you might say, "I can see that you're feeling sad right now," or "It sounds like you're really frustrated."

2. Express Understanding and Support: Express genuine understanding and support for the child's emotions. Let the child know that it's normal and okay to feel the way they do, and that you are there to listen and help them navigate their feelings. Offer words of encouragement and reassurance, emphasizing that their feelings are valid and worthy of attention.

3. Validate the Child's Experience: Validate the child's experience by affirming the significance of their feelings and experiences. Let the child know that their emotions matter and that you are taking them seriously. Avoid minimizing or dismissing the child's emotions, as this can undermine their sense of self-worth and confidence in expressing their feelings.

4. Use Empathetic Language: Choose your words carefully to convey empathy and compassion towards the child's emotions. Use empathetic language that reflects your understanding and support for their feelings. For example, you might say, "It's okay to feel angry," or "I understand why you're feeling disappointed."

5. Offer Comfort and Reassurance: Provide comfort and reassurance to the child by offering physical affection, such as a hug or a gentle touch, if appropriate. Let the child know that you are there to support them and help them feel better. Offer words of comfort and encouragement, letting the child know that they are not alone in their emotions.

6. Encourage Emotional Expression: Encourage the child to express their emotions openly and honestly, without fear of judgment or criticism. Create a safe and supportive environment where the child feels comfortable sharing their feelings. Validate the child's courage and vulnerability in expressing their emotions, and let them know that their feelings are valued and respected.

7. Listen Attentively: Listen attentively to the child's words and nonverbal cues, showing that you are fully present and engaged in the conversation. Give the child your undivided attention and avoid distractions or interruptions. Demonstrate active listening by validating the child's emotions and responding with empathy and compassion.

Normalize Emotions:

Normalizing emotions is essential for helping children understand that their feelings are valid and understandable reactions to loss and change. By reassuring children that it's okay to feel sad, angry, or confused, caregivers can create a supportive environment where children feel accepted and understood. Here are practical ways to normalize emotions and promote emotional well-being in children:

1. Validate Common Feelings: Acknowledge and validate the emotions commonly associated with loss and change, such as sadness, anger, confusion, and fear. Let children know that it's normal and natural to experience a range of emotions during challenging times, and that their feelings are valid and worthy of attention.

2. Provide Examples: Offer examples of common emotions and experiences to help children understand that they are not alone in their feelings. Share stories or anecdotes from your own life or from books and media that illustrate how people of all ages and backgrounds experience similar emotions in response to loss and change.

3. Normalize Emotional Expression: Encourage children to express their emotions openly and honestly, without fear of judgment or criticism. Let them know that it's healthy and normal to talk about their feelings and that bottling up emotions can lead to greater distress. Normalize emotional expression as a natural and necessary part of processing emotions and healing from loss.

4. Share Coping Strategies: Provide children with coping strategies and techniques for managing difficult emotions in healthy ways. Teach them relaxation techniques, mindfulness practices, and creative outlets for expressing their feelings. Normalize the use of coping strategies as helpful tools for navigating emotions and promoting emotional well-being.

5. Model Emotional Regulation: Model healthy emotional regulation skills by managing your own emotions in constructive ways. Demonstrate how to identify, express, and cope with emotions effectively, showing children that it's possible to navigate difficult feelings with resilience and grace. Normalize the practice of self-care and seeking support from others when needed.

6. Encourage Self-Compassion: Encourage children to practice self-compassion and kindness towards themselves when experiencing difficult emotions. Normalize the idea that it's okay to be gentle with oneself during times of struggle and to seek comfort and support from caregivers and loved ones. Teach children to offer themselves the same understanding and compassion they would extend to others.

7. Foster a Culture of Acceptance: Create a culture of acceptance and understanding where children feel safe and supported in expressing their emotions authentically. Normalize the idea that everyone experiences emotions differently and that there is no right or wrong way to feel. Celebrate emotional diversity and encourage children to embrace their feelings as valuable aspects of their inner lives.

Encourage Expression:

Encouraging children to express their feelings is vital for promoting emotional well-being and fostering healthy coping mechanisms. By creating opportunities for children to share their thoughts and emotions through various mediums, caregivers can help them process their feelings and develop effective ways of managing them. Here are practical ways to encourage expression in children:

1. Provide Art Supplies: Offer a variety of art supplies, such as crayons, markers, paints, and paper, to inspire children to express themselves creatively. Encourage them to create drawings, paintings, or collages that reflect their emotions and experiences. Art allows children to express complex feelings in a tangible and symbolic way, providing a sense of catharsis and empowerment.

2. Journaling or Writing Prompts: Introduce journaling or writing prompts to prompt children to explore their thoughts and emotions through writing. Provide notebooks or journals where children can write freely about their feelings, experiences, and reflections. Journaling allows children to process their emotions, gain insight into their inner world, and track their emotional journey over time.

3. Role-Playing and Pretend Play: Encourage children to engage in role-playing or pretend play activities that allow them to act out scenarios related to their feelings and experiences. Provide props, costumes, or puppets to enhance imaginative play and encourage children to express themselves through storytelling and dramatic play.

Role-playing enables children to explore different perspectives and emotions in a safe and creative environment.

4. Open-Ended Conversations: Initiate open-ended conversations with children to encourage them to share their thoughts and emotions freely. Create a safe and nonjudgmental space where children feel comfortable expressing themselves without fear of criticism or rejection. Listen attentively to their words and validate their experiences, offering comfort and support as needed.

5. Storytelling and Storybooks: Use storytelling and storybooks as tools for exploring emotions and fostering empathy in children. Read books that address themes of loss, change, or difficult emotions, and engage children in discussions about the characters' feelings and experiences. Encourage children to relate the stories to their own lives and share their thoughts and emotions inspired by the narratives.

6. Sensory Play: Engage children in sensory play activities that stimulate their senses and provide opportunities for emotional expression. Offer sensory materials such as playdough, sand, water, or sensory bins filled with various textures and objects. Sensory play allows children to explore and process their emotions through tactile experiences and sensory exploration.

7. Respect Autonomy and Choice: Respect children's autonomy and choice in how they choose to express their feelings. Allow them to select the mediums and activities that resonate with them and empower them to express themselves authentically. Avoid imposing specific forms of expression and instead encourage children to follow their interests and intuition.

Validate Nonverbal Cues:

Paying attention to children's nonverbal cues is essential for understanding their emotions and providing effective support and validation. Nonverbal communication, including facial expressions, body language, and tone of voice, can offer valuable insights into children's feelings and experiences. By validating children's nonverbal signals with empathy and reassurance, caregivers can create a supportive environment where children feel understood and accepted. Here are practical ways to validate nonverbal cues in children:

1. **Observe Facial Expressions:** Take note of children's facial expressions, as they often provide clues about their emotional state. Notice changes in their expressions, such as furrowed brows, downturned mouths, or widened eyes, which may indicate feelings of sadness, frustration, or excitement. Validate children's facial expressions by reflecting back what you see and acknowledging their emotions with empathy.

2. **Interpret Body Language:** Pay attention to children's body language, including posture, gestures, and movements, to gain insight into their emotional experiences. Notice if children are slouching, fidgeting, or avoiding eye contact, which may suggest discomfort, anxiety, or agitation. Validate children's body language by responding sensitively to their cues and offering support and reassurance.

3. **Listen to Tone of Voice:** Listen to children's tone of voice and vocal cues, as they can convey subtle nuances of emotion and mood. Notice changes in their tone, volume, or pitch, which may reflect underlying feelings of sadness, anger, or excitement. Validate children's tone of voice by acknowledging their emotional expression and responding with empathy and understanding.

4. Reflect Emotions Back: Reflect children's nonverbal cues back to them to demonstrate that you are attuned to their feelings and experiences. Use empathetic statements to mirror their emotions, such as "I can see that you're feeling upset" or "It looks like you're feeling excited." By validating children's nonverbal signals, caregivers show that they are present and engaged in understanding their emotional world.

5. Offer Reassurance and Support: Provide reassurance and support in response to children's nonverbal cues, offering comfort and validation for their emotions. Use gentle touch, comforting words, and empathetic gestures to convey your understanding and acceptance of their feelings. Let children know that it's okay to feel the way they do and that you are there to support them through their emotional experiences.

6. Create a Safe Space for Expression: Create a safe and nonjudgmental environment where children feel comfortable expressing their emotions through nonverbal cues. Encourage open communication and emotional expression, validating children's signals without criticism or judgment. Foster trust and connection by honoring children's nonverbal cues and responding with empathy and support.

7. Practice Active Observation: Practice active observation by tuning into children's nonverbal cues during everyday interactions and activities. Be attentive and present in the moment, noticing subtle changes in children's behavior and demeanor. Use your observations to guide your responses and validate children's emotions with sensitivity and compassion.

Chapter 5: The Language of Emotions:

142

Helping Your Child Understand and Express Their Feelings

In the hustle and bustle of daily life, it's not uncommon for children to experience moments of emotional overwhelm or confusion. Picture this: you're in a crowded store, and suddenly your child becomes inconsolable, melting down in the middle of the aisle. Despite your attempts to comfort them, they seem unable to articulate what's wrong, leaving you feeling helpless and frustrated. Scenes like these are all too familiar for many parents, highlighting the importance of emotional literacy in children's healthy development.

Emotional intelligence, often referred to as EQ, is the ability to recognize, understand, and manage one's own emotions, as well as to empathize with the emotions of others. It encompasses a range of skills, including self-awareness, self-regulation, motivation, empathy, and social skills. These core components form the foundation of emotional intelligence and play a crucial role in children's overall well-being and success in life.

Perhaps you've encountered similar scenarios: a tearful outburst during a playdate, a frustrated tantrum over a seemingly trivial matter, or a withdrawn silence in response to a challenging situation. In moments like these, parents confront the profound challenge of understanding and addressing their child's emotions, underscoring the critical importance of emotional literacy in nurturing healthy development.

In this chapter, we'll explore how parents can help their children develop emotional intelligence by teaching them the language of emotions. By fostering emotional awareness, empathy, and effective communication, parents can empower their children to navigate their inner world with confidence and resilience.

Practical Strategies for Teaching Children about Emotions

Building Emotional Vocabulary:

One of the fundamental steps in helping children understand and express their emotions is by building their emotional vocabulary. By introducing a wide range of emotions beyond the basic happy and sad, parents can empower children to articulate their feelings with greater precision and clarity. Here are some practical strategies to enrich your child's emotional vocabulary:

1. **Introduce a wide range of emotions:**

Encourage your child to explore a diverse spectrum of emotions by introducing words like frustrated, excited, nervous, proud, disappointed, and silly. Engage in conversations about daily experiences and help them label their feelings using these descriptive terms. For example, "I noticed you were feeling frustrated when you couldn't find your favorite toy."

1. **Read books with emotional themes:**

Storytelling provides a powerful platform for children to connect with emotions in relatable contexts. Choose books with characters experiencing a range of emotions and discuss these feelings with your child as you read together. Ask questions like, "How do you think the character feels right now?" or "Have you ever felt like this before?"

1. **Play emotion charades:**

Turn learning about emotions into a fun and interactive game by playing emotion charades. Take turns acting out different emotions using facial expressions and body language, while your child guesses the feeling. This activity not only reinforces emotional recognition but also encourages empathy and perspective-taking.

Here's how to play a fun game of emotion charades with your child:

Preparation:

❖ **Gather Players:** You can play this game with just two people (you and your child) or with a larger group (family game night!).

❖ **Decide on Acting or Describing:** For younger children, acting out emotions might be easier. For older children, you can introduce an additional challenge by describing the emotion with words (without using the actual emotion word) or using sounds.

❖ **Optional Props:** If you want to add some variety, you can have a hat with emotion words written on slips of paper, or pictures of faces showing different emotions.

Playing the Game:

❖ **Take Turns Acting/Describing:**

o If acting, choose an emotion (secretly if playing with a group) and act it out without speaking.

o If describing, use words or sounds to convey the emotion without saying the actual word.

❖ **Guessing:**

o The other players take turns guessing the emotion you're acting out or describing.

o Encourage silly guesses and celebrate creativity!

❖ **Pointing and Labeling:** Once the emotion is guessed correctly, you can point to an emotion chart (if you have one) and label the feeling together.

❖ **Switch Roles:** Once you've finished your turn, it's your child's turn to act out or describe an emotion!

Adding Fun Twists:

❖ **Time Limit:** Set a timer for an extra challenge. The player with the most correct guesses within the time limit wins.

❖ **Themed Rounds:** Choose a theme for each round, like emotions in stories or emotions during specific activities (e.g., emotions at the playground).

❖ **Team Play:** For larger groups, divide into teams and take turns acting out or describing emotions. The first team to guess correctly scores a point.

Benefits of Emotion Charades:

❖ **Learning Through Play:** This game is a fun way for children to identify and express different emotions.

❖ **Building Vocabulary:** As you play, discuss different emotion words and their meanings.

❖ **Enhancing Communication Skills:** Children learn to communicate nonverbally through acting and interpret nonverbal cues while guessing.

❖ **Family Bonding:** It's a simple and engaging activity that can bring laughter and connection.

Remember, the key is to have fun and create a positive atmosphere where your child feels comfortable expressing themselves.

1. Create an emotion chart:

Visual aids can be valuable tools for young children to grasp abstract concepts like emotions. Create an emotion chart using pictures or simple words to visually represent different emotions. Hang the chart in a prominent place in your home and encourage your child to point to or discuss how they're feeling throughout the day. This visual reference can serve as a helpful reminder and conversation starter for exploring emotions together.

Here's an example of a simple emotion chart you can create with your child:

Title: My Feelings Chart

Use: Drawings or pictures (for younger children) or a combination of drawings and words (for older children)

Emotions:

❖ **Happy:** Use a picture of a smiling face with sunshine in the background.

❖ **Sad:** Use a picture of a frowning face with a rainy cloud above it.

❖ **Angry:** Use a picture of a face with furrowed brows and a clenched mouth, perhaps with red squiggly lines for anger.

❖ **Scared:** Use a picture of a face with wide eyes and a worried expression.

❖ **Surprised:** Use a picture of a face with raised eyebrows and an open mouth.

❖ **Calm:** Use a picture of a peaceful face with a closed mouth and a relaxed posture.

You can also add more complex emotions as your child develops their emotional vocabulary, such as:

❖ Frustrated

❖ Excited

❖ Proud

❖ Disappointed

❖ Silly

❖ Confused

Here are some tips for using the emotion chart:

❖ **Create it together:** Let your child participate in choosing pictures or drawing faces for the chart. This will make them more invested in using it.

❖ **Point to the chart:** When your child expresses an emotion, point to the corresponding picture on the chart and name the feeling.

❖ **Use it during playtime:** Talk about how characters in stories or pretend play might be feeling and use the chart as a reference.

❖ **Hang it in a visible location:** This will serve as a reminder for your child to identify and express their emotions.

Remember, this is just a basic example. You can customize the chart to fit your child's age and interests.

Everyday Learning Opportunities:

Emotional intelligence isn't just developed in structured lessons or formal settings; it thrives in the everyday moments of life. As parents, we have the unique opportunity to create a nurturing environment where our children can learn about emotions through daily interactions and experiences. Here are some practical strategies to seize everyday learning opportunities and cultivate emotional intelligence in your child:

1. Narrate your own emotions:

Throughout the day, take the time to openly share and verbalize your own emotions with your child. Whether you're feeling stressed about a looming deadline, excited about an upcoming family outing, or frustrated by a minor inconvenience, narrating your emotions aloud helps demystify the process of emotional expression. By modeling healthy emotional communication, you not only demonstrate the normalcy of feeling a range of emotions but also provide valuable insight into coping strategies. For instance, you might say, "I feel overwhelmed with this mess, but taking a deep breath helps me feel calmer and more focused."

2. Label your child's emotions:

When your child expresses an emotion, whether through words, actions, or body language, take the time to acknowledge and validate their feelings. By labeling their emotions, you help them develop a rich emotional vocabulary and enhance their capacity for self-awareness. For example, if your child is struggling to reach a toy and becomes visibly frustrated, you might say, "It sounds like you're feeling frustrated because you can't reach that toy. That must be really frustrating. Let's see if we can find a way to help you."

3. Talk about emotions in stories and shows:

Storytelling provides a powerful platform for exploring emotions in relatable contexts. As you read books or watch shows with your child, pause periodically to discuss the emotions of the characters and how they might be feeling in different situations. Encourage your child to empathize with the characters and consider their perspectives. By engaging in these conversations, you not only deepen your child's understanding of emotions but also strengthen their capacity for empathy and perspective-taking. For instance, you might say, "How do you think the character feels right now? Can you think of a time when you felt similar emotions?"

By integrating these everyday learning opportunities into your daily routine, you create a supportive environment where your child can develop essential emotional intelligence skills. Through open communication, empathy, and reflection, you lay the groundwork for a lifetime of healthy emotional expression and resilience.

Creative Expression:

Creative activities provide a unique and powerful outlet for children to explore and express their emotions in a safe and constructive manner. Through art, storytelling, music, and movement, children can unleash their imagination, deepen their understanding of emotions, and develop essential skills for emotional expression. Here are some creative expression activities to engage your child and nurture their emotional intelligence:

1. Art projects:

Encourage your child to engage in drawing, painting, or sculpting as a means of exploring and expressing their emotions. Provide a variety of art materials and encourage them to create freely, without judgment or expectation. As they work on their art projects, engage in open-ended conversations about the emotions their artwork might represent. Ask questions like, "What emotions do you think your painting captures?" or "How did you choose the colors to express your feelings?"

2. Storytelling:

Harness the power of storytelling to engage your child's imagination and foster emotional exploration. Collaborate on creating stories together, where characters navigate different emotions and experiences. Encourage your child to invent characters, settings, and plotlines that reflect a range of emotions, from joy and excitement to fear and sadness. As you craft stories together, discuss the emotions of the characters and how they respond to challenges and conflicts.

3. Music and movement:

Music has a profound effect on our emotions and can serve as a powerful tool for emotional expression and regulation. Encourage your child to explore different types of music and engage in movement activities that reflect various emotions. Play upbeat, energetic music for happy emotions and slower, more soothing music for sad or contemplative emotions. As you listen to music together, discuss how the music makes you feel and encourage your child to express their own emotional responses through movement, dance, or creative play.

By providing opportunities for creative expression, you empower your child to explore and express their emotions in meaningful and authentic ways. Through art, storytelling, music, and movement, children not only deepen their emotional awareness but also develop important skills for self-expression, empathy, and communication. Embrace the power of creativity as a gateway to emotional discovery and growth in your child's journey towards emotional intelligence.

Play and Games:

Play is the language of childhood, offering children a natural and enjoyable way to explore the world around them and develop essential skills, including emotional intelligence. Through imaginative play, games, and interactive activities, children can deepen their understanding of emotions, practice empathy, and enhance their social skills. Here are some playful ideas to incorporate into your child's routine:

1. Pretend play:

Encourage your child to engage in pretend play, where they can immerse themselves in imaginary scenarios and experiment with expressing a range of emotions in a safe and supportive environment. Provide props, costumes, and open-ended prompts to inspire creative play. Whether they're pretending to be a doctor comforting a patient or a superhero saving the day, encourage your child to explore different emotions and perspectives through their imaginative play.

2. Emotion matching games:

Engage your child in interactive games that challenge them to recognize and match emotions with corresponding facial expressions or emotion words. Create a set of cards featuring pictures of faces displaying different emotions, such as happiness, sadness, anger, and surprise. Then, invite your child to match each face with the corresponding emotion word. This activity not only strengthens their emotional recognition skills but also promotes vocabulary development and empathy.

3. "Guess the feeling" games:

This is similar to emotional charades discussed above. You need to turn emotional exploration into a fun and engaging game by playing "Guess the feeling" with your child. Take turns describing different scenarios or situations and have your child guess the emotion someone might feel in that moment. For example, you might say, "Imagine you're waiting to perform in a school talent show. How do you think you would feel?" Encourage your child to consider a range of emotions and perspectives, fostering empathy and perspective-taking skills.

By incorporating playful activities and games into your child's daily routine, you provide valuable opportunities for them to learn about emotions, practice social skills, and strengthen their emotional intelligence. Through imaginative play, interactive games, and creative exploration, children can develop a deeper understanding of themselves and others, laying the foundation for healthy emotional development and positive relationships.

Creating a Safe Space:

A safe and supportive environment is essential for nurturing children's emotional well-being and fostering healthy emotional expression. By creating a safe space where children feel valued, heard, and understood, caregivers can empower children to navigate their emotions with confidence and resilience. Here are some strategies to establish a safe space for your child to explore and express their emotions:

1. Open communication:

Encourage your child to talk about their feelings openly and honestly, without fear of judgment or criticism. Create opportunities for meaningful conversations by actively listening to their thoughts, concerns, and experiences. Let them know that you're always there to listen and support them, no matter what emotions they're experiencing.

2. Set clear boundaries:

Establish clear boundaries around acceptable behavior while validating your child's emotions. Let them know that it's okay to feel angry, frustrated, or upset, but it's not okay to hurt themselves or others. Teach them healthy ways to express and cope with their emotions, such as using words to communicate their feelings or taking a break to cool down when they're upset.

3. Respect their privacy:

Give your child space and autonomy to express their emotions on their own terms. Respect their need for privacy and independence while remaining available and supportive when they need you. Create designated areas in your home where your child can retreat to when they need time alone to process their emotions.

4. Respond calmly to emotional outbursts:

When your child experiences emotional outbursts, respond with patience, empathy, and understanding. Stay calm and collected, even when faced with challenging behavior, and avoid reacting impulsively or harshly. Validate your child's feelings by acknowledging their emotions and offering comfort and support. Help them find healthy ways to calm down, such as deep breathing, taking a walk, or engaging in a calming activity.

By creating a safe space where children feel respected, supported, and understood, caregivers can empower children to navigate their emotions with confidence and resilience. Through open communication, clear boundaries, respect for privacy, and calm, compassionate responses, caregivers can foster a nurturing environment where children can thrive emotionally and develop essential skills for lifelong well-being.

Cultural Considerations Around Emotions

Emotions are not only universal but also deeply influenced by cultural norms, beliefs, and practices. It's essential to acknowledge and respect the diversity of cultural perspectives on emotions, as they shape how individuals experience, express, and perceive feelings. Understanding cultural considerations around emotions is crucial for parents and caregivers, as it enables them to support children's emotional development in culturally sensitive and inclusive ways. Here are some key points to consider:

Acknowledge the Diversity of Cultural Norms Around Emotions:

Cultures vary widely in their attitudes toward emotions, with some placing a high value on emotional expressiveness and others emphasizing restraint or stoicism. Recognize that there is no one-size-fits-all approach to emotions and that cultural norms play a significant role in shaping how emotions are understood and expressed.

While a frown might universally signal sadness, the way we experience, express, and even perceive emotions can vary greatly across cultures. It's important to acknowledge this diversity as we navigate the world of emotions with our children.

A Tapestry of Expression:

 ❖ **Open Cultures:** Some cultures encourage open and outward displays of emotion. Tears, laughter, and even anger might be freely expressed. In these cultures, children may be comfortable readily sharing their feelings and using strong facial expressions.

❖ **Stoic Cultures:** In contrast, other cultures may emphasize emotional control and restraint. Outward displays of strong emotions might be seen as disrespectful or disruptive. Children raised in these cultures may learn to manage their emotions more subtly, focusing on internal processing rather than external expression.

Understanding the Why:

These cultural differences stem from various factors, including:

❖ **Historical Background:** A culture's history of conflict or hardship might influence the value placed on emotional control.

❖ **Social Harmony:** Some cultures prioritize maintaining social harmony, and expressing strong emotions might be seen as disruptive to that balance.

❖ **Religious Beliefs:** Religious teachings can influence how emotions are perceived and managed.

Navigating the Nuances:

❖ **Respectful Communication:** As parents, it's crucial to be mindful of our own cultural background and how it shapes our approach to emotions.

❖ **Embrace Differences:** When encountering children from diverse backgrounds, celebrate the richness of emotional expression and avoid judging unfamiliar displays of emotions.

❖ **Open Dialogue:** Talk to your child about cultural differences in emotional expression. Explore how emotions are portrayed in movies, books, or music from various cultures.

❖ **Focus on Universals:** Despite cultural variations, some core emotions like happiness, sadness, and fear are likely to be experienced universally.

Remember: There's no single "correct" way to express emotions. Our goal is to help children become emotionally intelligent, and that includes understanding and respecting the diversity of emotional expression across cultures.

Cultural Background Influences on Emotional Expression and Perception:

Cultural background profoundly influences how individuals learn to express and interpret emotions. Some cultures may encourage open and direct expression of feelings, while others may value emotional restraint or modesty. Discuss with children how their cultural background shapes their understanding of emotions and how they express themselves.

The world of emotions is as colorful and diverse as the cultures that inhabit it. While a joyful laugh or a tear of sadness might seem universal, the way we experience, express, and even understand these emotions can be influenced significantly by our cultural background. Let's delve deeper into how culture shapes our emotional landscape:

The Expressive Spectrum:

❖ **Open Expression:** In some cultures, emotions are worn on the sleeve. People openly express joy, anger, or frustration through laughter, tears, or animated body language. Children raised in these cultures might be comfortable readily sharing their feelings and using strong facial expressions. Imagine a lively Italian family dinner where laughter and passionate discussions intertwine!

❖ **Subtle Expression:** On the other hand, some cultures place a high value on emotional control and subtlety. Outward displays of strong emotions might be seen as disrespectful or disruptive. Children from these cultures might learn to manage their emotions more internally, focusing on calming techniques or expressing themselves indirectly. Think about a Japanese tea ceremony where tranquility and composure are emphasized.

Why the Differences?

These cultural variations in emotional expression stem from various reasons:

❖ **Historical and Social Context:** A culture's history of conflict or hardship might influence the importance placed on emotional control. Conversely, a culture that prioritizes social harmony might discourage outbursts to maintain a peaceful environment.

❖ **Religious Beliefs:** Religious teachings and practices can shape how emotions are perceived and managed. Some religions might emphasize stoicism and acceptance, while others encourage outward expressions of devotion.

❖ **Family Values:** Family dynamics and upbringing play a crucial role. Children raised in a household that openly discusses emotions will likely feel comfortable expressing themselves freely compared to a household that values emotional restraint.

Exploring with Your Child:

❖ **Open Communication:** Talk to your child about how your family expresses emotions. Share stories about your own cultural background and how it may have influenced your emotional expression.

❖ **Cultural Exploration:** Explore different cultures together through books, movies, or music. Discuss how emotions are portrayed in these different contexts.

❖ **Embrace Diversity:** Help your child understand that there's no single "correct" way to express emotions. Celebrate the richness of cultural expression and encourage them to be respectful of how others express their feelings.

Remember: By fostering an awareness of cultural differences in emotional expression, you equip your child with valuable tools for navigating the world with empathy and understanding. They'll learn to appreciate the diversity of emotions while developing their own healthy ways of expressing themselves.

Navigating Cultural Differences in Emotional Expression:

When parenting children from diverse cultural backgrounds, it's essential to respect and honor their cultural heritage. Encourage open dialogue about emotions and cultural practices surrounding them. Be mindful of cultural differences in communication styles, body language, and nonverbal cues. Emphasize the importance of accepting and validating children's emotions, regardless of cultural norms.

Our world is a vibrant tapestry of cultures, each with its unique way of understanding and expressing emotions. As parents raising children from diverse backgrounds, it's important to cultivate an environment that respects and celebrates this rich tapestry. Here are some tips for navigating cultural differences in emotional expression:

- **Embrace Open Dialogue:** Foster a safe space where your child feels comfortable talking about their emotions. Encourage them to share their experiences and how their cultural background might influence their feelings. Actively listen without judgment and ask open-ended questions to deepen understanding.

- **Explore Cultural Practices:** Take an interest in your child's cultural heritage. Explore books, movies, or traditional practices that shed light on how emotions are viewed and expressed within their culture. Discuss how these practices might differ from your own cultural background.

- **Mind the Nonverbal Cues:** Be mindful that communication styles, body language, and nonverbal cues can vary significantly across cultures. A raised eyebrow might signal annoyance in one culture, while in another, it could be a question mark. Learn about common nonverbal expressions in your child's cultural background to avoid misinterpretations.

- **Focus on Validation:** Emphasize the importance of acknowledging and validating your child's emotions, regardless of how they express them. Remember, cultural norms don't erase the legitimacy of feelings. Let your child know their emotions are valid, even if the cultural expectation might be for more subtle expression.

❖ **Seek Resources:** Consider seeking resources or connecting with professionals who specialize in cultural competency. This can provide valuable insights and strategies for navigating emotional expression within a diverse family.

❖ **Celebrate Differences:** Instead of viewing cultural differences as challenges, celebrate them as opportunities for growth and learning. Use them as a chance to teach your child about empathy and understanding for people from all walks of life.

❖ **Be a Bridge:** When encountering situations where cultural clashes might arise due to emotional expression, act as a bridge. Help your child understand the expectations of the other culture while advocating for their right to express their emotions authentically, within social boundaries.

By following these tips, you can create a nurturing environment where your child feels comfortable exploring their emotions while appreciating the beautiful diversity of emotional expression in the world. Remember, the goal is to raise an emotionally intelligent child who can navigate the world with empathy, respect, and a healthy understanding of their own feelings.

Microaggressions and their Impact on Emotional Well-being:

Microaggressions are subtle, often unintentional acts of discrimination or prejudice that can have a significant impact on a child's emotional well-being. Help children recognize and understand microaggressions, and teach them strategies for coping with and confronting such experiences. Foster an environment of inclusivity, respect, and acceptance, where all children feel valued and supported.

In our journey to raise emotionally intelligent children, we must address the subtle yet potent influence of microaggressions. These seemingly minor instances of prejudice or discrimination, often unintentional, can chip away at a child's self-esteem and emotional well-being. Here's how we can navigate this challenge:

Understanding Microaggressions:

❖ **Invisible Cuts:** Microaggressions are like tiny cuts - subtle, sometimes unnoticed by the perpetrator, but leaving a lasting sting on the recipient. They can be verbal (comments about appearance or cultural background), behavioral (dismissive actions), or environmental (stereotypical portrayals in media).

❖ **Impact on Children:** These seemingly insignificant acts can have a significant impact on a child's emotional well-being. They can lead to feelings of isolation, confusion, anger, and even internalized prejudice.

Empowering Your Child:

❖ **Recognition is Key:** Help your child recognize microaggressions. Discuss common examples and how they might make them feel. Role-play scenarios to equip them with the ability to identify such situations.

❖ **Coping Strategies:** Teach your child healthy coping mechanisms. Encourage them to express their feelings openly to you or a trusted adult. Deep breathing exercises or journaling can help them manage the emotional impact.

❖ **Confrontation (Optional):** Depending on the situation and your child's comfort level, you can discuss strategies for gentle confrontation. Encourage them to politely point out the microaggression and its effect. Role-playing assertive responses can be helpful.

Building a Safe Space:

❖ **Open Communication:** Create a safe space where your child feels comfortable talking about any microaggressions they experience. Listen attentively and validate their feelings.

❖ **Empowerment Through Knowledge:** Discuss diversity, equity, and inclusion (DEI) with your child. Teach them about different cultures and backgrounds. The more they understand, the better equipped they are to navigate a diverse world.

❖ **Role Modeling Respect:** Be mindful of your own language and behavior. Avoid stereotypes and microaggressions in your interactions. Show your child how to treat others with respect and acceptance.

Fostering Inclusivity:

❖ **Inclusive Environment:** Surround your child with diverse books, movies, and role models. Celebrate the richness of different cultures and backgrounds.

❖ **Community Connections:** Seek out inclusive activities and communities for your child. This fosters a sense of belonging and acceptance within a diverse group.

Remember: Addressing microaggressions requires a multi-pronged approach. By empowering your child with knowledge, coping strategies, and a safe space for communication, you can help them navigate these challenges and build emotional resilience. Ultimately, we strive to create a world where all children feel valued and respected, fostering a future where microaggressions become a thing of the past.

Part 3: Mindful Parenting through the Stages

Chapter 6: The Early Years (Birth to 5)

Introduction:

In the soft glow of dawn, a newborn's cry fills the room, signaling the start of a journey filled with wonder, joy, and challenges. From the first moments of life to the vibrant explorations of toddlerhood, the early years encompass a time of rapid growth and development. As parents, we are entrusted with the precious task of nurturing our young children, guiding them through the milestones and magic of infancy and early childhood. In this chapter, we will explore the unique joys and challenges of parenting during the early years, from building secure attachment to fostering emotional resilience. Through mindful parenting practices, we can lay a strong foundation for our children's future well-being and happiness.

The Emotional Landscape:

During the early years, children embark on a journey of emotional discovery, experiencing a kaleidoscope of feelings as they navigate the world around them. From the gurgles of infant delight to the tears of frustration in toddlerhood, young children begin to explore and express a range of emotions, including happiness, sadness, anger, fear, and excitement. As they learn to interpret facial expressions, vocal cues, and body language, they develop the building blocks of emotional intelligence. By nurturing their emotional awareness and vocabulary, we empower our children to navigate their inner world with confidence and resilience.

Mindful Parenting Strategies:

In the gentle embrace of mindful parenting, we discover a wealth of strategies to support our children's emotional development during the early years. Through responsive caregiving and sensitive listening, we cultivate secure attachment bonds that provide a foundation of trust and safety. We incorporate mindfulness practices into our daily routines, from soothing bedtime rituals to playful sensory experiences, helping our children regulate their emotions and find calm amidst the chaos. By embracing positive discipline approaches rooted in empathy and understanding, we teach our children valuable lessons in empathy, cooperation, and self-control. Through storytelling, music, and imaginative play, we create rich opportunities for emotional expression and exploration, nurturing our children's creativity and self-expression.

Addressing Common Challenges:

As parents navigating the early years, we may encounter common concerns and challenges along the way. From sleepless nights to tearful goodbyes, we grapple with the complexities of sleep issues and separation anxiety, seeking solace in soothing bedtime routines and gradual transitions. We strive to foster independence and self-confidence in our young children, while providing a secure and nurturing environment that encourages exploration and growth. Through gentle guidance and consistent routines, we navigate the ebbs and flows of early childhood, embracing each challenge as an opportunity for connection and growth.

The early years lay the foundation for a child's emotional well-being. While this period is filled with wonder and joy, it can also present challenges for both children and parents. Here' are some of the common concerns parents might face during this crucial stage:

❖ **Sleep Issues:** Sleep patterns vary greatly throughout early childhood. Newborns might wake frequently for feedings, while toddlers may resist bedtime or struggle with nightmares. Parents might face challenges establishing consistent sleep routines.

❖ **Separation Anxiety:** Around 8 months, separation anxiety often peaks. Infants and young children may become distressed when separated from their primary caregivers. This can make errands, daycare drop-offs, or even short goodbyes difficult.

❖ **Tantrums and Meltdowns:** Young children often lack the vocabulary and emotional regulation skills to express themselves effectively. This can lead to frustration and meltdowns, particularly during transitions or when they don't get what they want.

❖ **Potty Training:** Potty training can be a long and messy process. Parents might face challenges with consistency, accidents, or resistance from their child.

❖ **Feeding Difficulties:** Some children may be picky eaters or go through phases of refusing certain foods. This can cause worry about their nutritional intake.

❖ **Sibling Rivalry:** The arrival of a new sibling can be a significant adjustment for a young child. Parents might face challenges managing jealousy, competition, and nurturing positive relationships between siblings.

❖ **Defiance and Limit-setting:** As toddlers gain independence, they may test boundaries and challenge rules. Parents need to develop effective strategies for setting clear limits and promoting positive behavior.

Navigating Challenges with Mindful Parenting

The early years are a whirlwind of growth and development. While this period is filled with incredible milestones, it can also present challenges for both children and parents. Here's how mindful parenting can help you navigate some common concerns in these early years:

Sleep Issues:

❖ **Develop a Consistent Routine:** Newborns thrive on predictability. Establish a bedtime routine that includes calming activities like baths, stories, and cuddles. Stick to consistent sleep and wake times as much as possible, even on weekends.

❖ **Create a Sleep-Promoting Environment:** Ensure the nursery is dark, quiet, and cool. Use calming white noise if needed.

❖ **Validate and Stay Calm:** It's natural for babies to fuss or cry at bedtime. Respond promptly but calmly. Offer comfort and reassurance without picking them up every time they stir.

❖ **Practice Self-Care:** A well-rested parent is a more patient parent. Prioritize your own sleep and relaxation whenever possible.

Separation Anxiety:

❖ **Gradual Goodbyes:** Don't disappear suddenly. Start by saying goodbye briefly within sight, then gradually extend the duration of your absence as your child tolerates it.

❖ **Practice Makes Perfect:** Role-play separations with stuffed animals or dolls. Let your child practice "waving goodbye" in a safe environment.

❖ **Comfort Objects:** Provide a familiar blanket or stuffed animal that can offer comfort when you're not around.

❖ **Stay Connected:** Leave a special note or picture in your child's bag. Let them know you'll be back soon and express your love.

Tantrums and Meltdowns:

❖ **Stay Calm:** A child's tantrum can be overwhelming, but avoid getting angry yourself. Take a deep breath and remember, this is a learning experience for them.

❖ **Validate Their Feelings:** Acknowledge their emotions by saying things like "I see you're feeling frustrated" or "It's okay to be angry."

❖ **Offer Choices When Possible:** During transitions, offer choices to give your child a sense of control. "Do you want to put on your red pajamas or the blue ones?"

❖ **Distraction is Key:** For younger children, try offering a distraction like a favorite toy or engaging in a silly song.

❖ **Focus on Solutions:** Once the tantrum has passed, help your child identify the emotion that triggered it and explore alternative solutions for expressing themselves in the future.

Potty Training:

❖ **Follow Your Child's Cues:** Don't start potty training too early. Look for signs of readiness like staying dry for longer periods or showing interest in the toilet.

❖ **Positive Reinforcement:** Celebrate successes with praise, stickers, or a high five. Avoid punishment for accidents, as this can create anxiety.

❖ **Be Patient and Consistent:** Accidents are inevitable. Stay calm, clean up messes without making a fuss, and offer gentle reminders to use the potty.

❖ **Make it Fun:** Invest in a colorful potty seat or fun books about potty training. Encourage your child to participate in choosing their underwear or training pants.

Feeding Difficulties:

❖ **Offer Choices and Control:** Provide a variety of healthy options and allow your child some control over what they eat. Let them choose between two different fruits or vegetables at mealtime.

❖ **Focus on Exposure, Not Pressure:** Don't force your child to eat something they dislike. Offer new foods repeatedly in a relaxed environment.

❖ **Lead by Example:** Model healthy eating habits yourself. Make mealtimes a positive social experience, not a battleground.

❖ **Focus on Playful Exploration:** Let your child explore food with their senses. Encourage them to touch, smell, and name different foods before they taste them.

Sibling Rivalry:

❖ **Spend Quality Time One-on-One:** Make time for each child individually. Let them have your undivided attention and enjoy special activities together.

❖ **Focus on Cooperation:** Encourage opportunities for siblings to play together cooperatively. Narrate their interactions and celebrate moments of sharing or kindness.

❖ **Positive Reinforcement:** Praise positive interactions between siblings. Offer rewards for acts of cooperation and sharing.

❖ **Validate Their Feelings:** Acknowledge jealousy or frustration expressed by either child. Let them know it's okay to feel those emotions, but offer helpful solutions for resolving conflict.

Defiance and Limit-Setting:

❖ **Set Clear and Consistent Limits:** Establish clear expectations and rules for behavior. Be consistent in enforcing them, even if it means saying no more often than you'd like.

❖ **Use Positive Reinforcement:** Catch your child being good! Praise them for following rules and positive behavior. This reinforces the desired behavior more effectively than focusing solely on punishment.

❖ **Offer Choices When Possible:** Provide opportunities for your child to make choices within safe boundaries. This fosters a sense of autonomy and reduces power struggles.

❖ **Natural Consequences:** When appropriate, allow natural consequences to unfold. For example, if your child refuses to wear a jacket, they might feel cold outside. Explain the connection between their choice and the outcome in a calm and matter-of-fact way.

❖ **Focus on Problem-Solving:** Instead of punishment, focus on finding solutions together. Help your child brainstorm ways to manage their emotions and make better choices next time.

Conclusion:

As we journey through the early years with our young children, we are reminded of the profound impact of mindful parenting on their emotional development and well-being. Through our nurturing presence and gentle guidance, we lay a strong foundation for their future happiness and success. Let us cherish the precious moments of infancy and early childhood, celebrating the milestones and marveling at the magic of this fleeting stage. With love, patience, and mindfulness, we empower our children to thrive in a world filled with boundless possibilities.

Chapter 7: The Middle Years (6 to 12)

Introduction:

As the sun rises on another day, children in the middle years awaken to a world of discovery and growth. Between the ages of 6 and 12, they embark on a journey of self-discovery, forging friendships, exploring new interests, and navigating the complexities of school and family life. In this chapter, we delve into the unique joys and challenges of parenting during the middle years, offering guidance and support to nurture our children's emotional intelligence and resilience.

The Emotional Landscape:

During the middle years, children experience a whirlwind of emotions as they navigate the transition from early childhood to adolescence. They grapple with the highs and lows of friendship dynamics, academic pressures, and burgeoning independence. From the excitement of new experiences to the frustration of setbacks, they learn to navigate a wide range of emotions, including joy, sadness, anger, anxiety, and pride. As they develop a deeper understanding of themselves and others, they begin to cultivate the seeds of emotional intelligence that will serve them well in the years to come.

Mindful Parenting Strategies:

In the midst of the middle years, mindful parenting offers a steady compass to guide us through the ups and downs of this transformative stage. We foster open and honest communication, creating a safe space for our children to express their thoughts and feelings without judgment. Through active listening and empathetic responses, we validate their experiences and offer support and guidance as they navigate the challenges of growing up. We model healthy coping mechanisms and self-regulation skills, demonstrating the power of mindfulness in managing stress and cultivating resilience. And we celebrate their achievements and milestones, nurturing their sense of self-worth and confidence as they navigate the journey of self-discovery.

Addressing Common Challenges:

As parents of children in the middle years, we encounter a host of common concerns and challenges along the way. From peer pressure and academic stress to conflicts with siblings and friends, we strive to provide guidance and support to help our children navigate these complexities with grace and resilience. We offer practical tips and strategies for fostering healthy friendships, managing time effectively, and coping with the demands of school and extracurricular activities. And we emphasize the importance of self-care and downtime, encouraging our children to prioritize their well-being amidst the busyness of life.

The middle years are a period of remarkable transformation. Children are developing a stronger sense of self, navigating the complexities of friendships, and embarking on their academic journey. While this stage is filled with exciting discoveries, it can also present some common concerns for parents:

- ❖ **Peer Pressure:** As children enter school and social circles expand, peer pressure becomes a growing influence. They may face pressure to conform, dress a certain way, or engage in risky behaviors.

- ❖ **Self-Esteem:** Self-awareness grows during this stage, and children become increasingly sensitive to their social standing and academic performance. This can lead to fluctuations in self-esteem and feelings of inadequacy.

- ❖ **Academic Challenges:** Schoolwork becomes more demanding, and some children may struggle with specific subjects or test anxiety. This can be frustrating and demotivating.

❖ **Friendship Issues:** Navigating friendships can be complex. Children may experience conflict, exclusion, or feelings of loneliness.

❖ **Bullying:** Unfortunately, bullying can be a reality for some children during this age group. It's important to be aware of the signs and offer support to your child.

❖ **Changes in Body Image:** As children approach puberty, their bodies begin to change. This can lead to self-consciousness and anxieties about physical development.

Navigating Challenges with Mindful Parenting

The middle years are a whirlwind of social, emotional, and academic development. While this age group is known for its boundless energy and curiosity, it can also be a time of challenges and vulnerabilities. Here's how mindful parenting can help you navigate some common concerns during this crucial stage:

Peer Pressure:

❖ **Open Communication:** Maintain open communication channels. Encourage your child to talk about their friendships and any peer pressure they might be facing.

❖ **Role-Playing Scenarios:** Practice saying no in different situations. Help them develop assertive communication skills to resist negative peer pressure.

❖ **Focus on Values:** Reinforce your family values and talk about the importance of making good choices, even when friends don't.

❖ **Build Self-Esteem:** A strong sense of self-worth makes children less susceptible to peer pressure. Encourage their interests and celebrate their individuality.

Self-Esteem:

❖ **Positive Reinforcement:** Catch your child being good! Focus on praise for their efforts, positive behaviors, and unique talents.

❖ **Focus on Progress, Not Perfection:** Acknowledge their hard work and celebrate improvement, even if they don't achieve perfect results.

❖ **Embrace Mistakes:** Mistakes are opportunities for learning. Help your child see them as stepping stones, not failures.

❖ **Body Positivity:** Promote a healthy body image. Talk about respecting all body types and focus on internal qualities like kindness and courage.

Academic Challenges:

❖ **Identify Learning Styles:** Understanding your child's learning style can be crucial. Explore different learning techniques and find approaches that work best for them.

❖ **Develop a Support System:** Work with teachers to identify areas needing improvement and develop a collaborative support plan. Consider a tutor or after-school program if needed.

❖ **Focus on Effort, Not Just Grades:** While grades are important, emphasize the value of effort, perseverance, and a love of learning.

❖ **Celebrate Small Wins:** Acknowledge and celebrate their progress, no matter how small. This keeps them motivated and builds confidence.

Friendship Issues:

❖ **Active Listening:** When your child faces friendship challenges, listen actively and validate their feelings. Avoid jumping in with solutions; let them express their emotions.

❖ **Social Skills Development:** Help your child develop strong social skills by encouraging empathy, cooperation, and conflict resolution techniques.

❖ **Expand Social Circles:** Encourage participation in extracurricular activities or clubs to broaden their social network.

❖ **Focus on Positive Friendships:** Nurture positive friendships and encourage interactions with kind and supportive peers.

Bullying:

❖ **Open Communication Channels:** Create a safe space for your child to talk about any bullying they might be experiencing.

❖ **Develop a Plan:** Work together to develop a plan if they encounter bullying. Encourage them to tell a trusted adult and practice assertive communication skills.

❖ **Empowerment and Support:** Assure your child you're there for them and will help them address the situation.

❖ **Seek Help if Needed:** Don't hesitate to reach out to teachers, counselors, or school administrators if the bullying is persistent or severe.

Changes in Body Image:

❖ **Open and Honest Communication:** Talk openly and honestly about puberty and body changes. Address their questions and concerns in an age-appropriate manner.

❖ **Challenge Stereotypes:** Counteract societal pressures surrounding body image by promoting a healthy and realistic view of beauty.

❖ **Focus on Inner Strength:** Help your child focus on their inner strengths, talents, and personality traits that make them unique.

❖ **Be a Role Model:** Practice body positivity yourself and avoid negative self-talk about your own appearance.

Conclusion:

As we journey through the middle years with our children, we are reminded of the profound impact of mindful parenting on their emotional well-being and development. Through our nurturing presence and supportive guidance, we empower them to navigate the challenges of this transformative stage with courage and resilience. Let us embrace the joys and complexities of the middle years, celebrating the milestones and cherishing the moments of connection and growth. With love, patience, and mindfulness, we lay a foundation for their future happiness and success.

Chapter 8: The Teenage Years (13 to 18+)

Introduction:

The teenage years herald a period of profound transformation as children transition into young adults, grappling with the complexities of identity, relationships, and independence. From the throes of adolescence to the brink of adulthood, this chapter explores the dynamic landscape of parenting teenagers, offering insights and strategies to navigate the challenges and opportunities of this pivotal stage.

The Emotional Landscape:

Adolescence is a rollercoaster of emotions, marked by the ebb and flow of joy, sorrow, excitement, and uncertainty. Teenagers navigate a whirlwind of developmental changes, from physical transformations to cognitive shifts and emotional upheavals. They grapple with questions of identity, belonging, and purpose, seeking to carve out their place in the world amidst the pressures of school, peers, and family expectations. As they wrestle with newfound freedoms and responsibilities, they experience a range of emotions, from the exhilaration of newfound autonomy to the angst of existential uncertainty.

Mindful Parenting Strategies:

In the midst of the teenage years, mindful parenting emerges as a beacon of support and guidance, offering a steady anchor amidst the stormy seas of adolescence. We foster open lines of communication, creating a safe space for our teenagers to express their thoughts and feelings without fear of judgment. Through active listening and empathetic responses, we validate their experiences and offer guidance and support as they navigate the challenges of adolescence. We model healthy coping mechanisms and self-regulation skills, demonstrating the power of mindfulness in managing stress and cultivating resilience. And we celebrate their achievements and milestones, nurturing their sense of self-worth and confidence as they navigate the journey of self-discovery.

Addressing Common Challenges:

Parenting teenagers comes with its own set of unique challenges and concerns, from peer pressure and academic stress to conflicts with siblings and struggles with identity and self-esteem. We offer practical strategies for fostering healthy communication and conflict resolution, helping our teenagers navigate the complexities of relationships and social dynamics. We provide guidance on setting boundaries and expectations, empowering our teenagers to make responsible choices and take ownership of their actions. And we emphasize the importance of self-care and self-compassion, supporting our teenagers as they navigate the ups and downs of adolescence with courage and resilience.

The teenage years are a period of immense change and emotional upheaval. Teenagers grapple with newfound independence, a surging desire for self-discovery, and the complexities of social relationships. Here are some additional common concerns parents might face during this often-tumultuous stage:

- **Conflict:** As teenagers strive for autonomy, disagreements and conflicts with parents become more frequent. These can range from arguments about curfews and chores to more serious clashes regarding values and life choices.

- **Setting Boundaries:** Finding the right balance between offering freedom and setting clear boundaries can be a challenge. Teenagers need guidance, but also opportunities to make their own decisions and learn from consequences.

- **Social Media:** Social media platforms can be a breeding ground for peer pressure, self-esteem issues, and exposure to inappropriate content. Navigating the digital world responsibly and setting healthy boundaries around screen time can be complex.

❖ **Risky Behaviors:** Teenagers are naturally prone to risk-taking behavior. This can include experimentation with drugs or alcohol, reckless driving, or engaging in unsafe sexual activity.

❖ **Academic Pressures:** Academic pressures intensify during these years, with college applications and future career paths looming large. Teenagers may experience stress, anxiety, or feelings of inadequacy regarding their academic performance.

❖ **Identity Exploration:** Teenagers grapple with questions about who they are, their values, and their place in the world. This can lead to experimentation with different styles, groups of friends, and even questioning their sexual orientation.

Navigating Challenges with Mindful Parenting

The teenage years are a whirlwind of emotions, identity exploration, and the constant push for independence. While this stage can be exhilarating for teenagers, it can also be a minefield for parents. Here's how mindful parenting can help you navigate some common concerns during these often-tumultuous years:

Conflict:

❖ **Pick Your Battles:** Not every disagreement needs to be a full-blown fight. Choose your battles wisely and focus on issues of safety, respect, and core values.

❖ **Active Listening:** When conflict arises, practice active listening. Listen attentively without interrupting, and acknowledge their feelings.

❖ **Focus on Problem-Solving:** Shift the focus from blame to problem-solving. Work together to brainstorm solutions that address everyone's concerns.

❖ **Validate Their Emotions:** Even if you disagree with their actions, acknowledge their emotions. Let them know its okay to feel frustrated or angry, but encourage them to express those feelings in a healthy way.

Setting Boundaries:

❖ **Collaborative Approach:** Instead of dictating rules, involve your teenager in setting boundaries. Discuss expectations, consequences, and the rationale behind the rules.

❖ **Focus on Flexibility:** Boundaries can be flexible and adapt as your teenager matures and demonstrates responsible behavior.

❖ **Open Communication:** Maintain open communication channels. Explain your reasoning behind boundaries and be willing to listen to their perspective.

❖ **Focus on the Why:** Help them understand the purpose of boundaries. It's not about control; it's about keeping them safe and helping them make responsible choices.

Social Media:

❖ **Open Dialogue:** Talk openly about the positive and negative aspects of social media. Discuss cyberbullying, privacy concerns, and the potential impact on self-esteem.

❖ **Lead by Example:** Model healthy social media habits yourself. Be mindful of your own screen time and avoid negativity online.

❖ **Set Ground Rules:** Work together to establish ground rules for social media use. This could include screen time limits, content restrictions, and responsible online behavior.

❖ **Promote Alternatives:** Encourage participation in activities and hobbies that offer a break from the digital world and foster face-to-face interactions.

Risky Behaviors:

❖ **Open Communication:** Maintain open and honest communication about risky behaviors. Create a safe space for your teenager to talk about peer pressure and their own anxieties.

❖ **Set Clear Expectations:** Express your expectations clearly and consistently regarding drugs, alcohol, and safe behavior.

❖ **Focus on the Consequences:** Discuss the potential consequences of risky behavior, focusing not just on punishment, but also on the real-life impact on their health and future.

❖ **Empowerment through Knowledge:** Equip your teenager with knowledge about the risks of substance abuse and unsafe practices.

Academic Pressures:

❖ **Focus on Effort and Progress:** Acknowledge their hard work and celebrate improvement over focusing solely on grades.

❖ **Develop Healthy Habits:** Encourage healthy sleep hygiene, organization skills, and time management techniques to combat stress and promote academic success.

❖ **Open Communication:** Maintain open communication about academic concerns. Offer support and help them find resources like tutors or study groups if needed.

❖ **Focus on Long-Term Goals:** Help them connect their academic efforts to their long-term goals and future aspirations.

Identity Exploration:

❖ **Create a Safe Space:** Create a safe and accepting environment where your teenager feels comfortable exploring their identity without judgment.

❖ **Active Listening:** Listen actively and express your support as they explore different styles, interests, and social circles.

❖ **Open Dialogue:** Encourage open dialogue about sexuality, gender identity, and other aspects of their evolving self-perception.

❖ **Be a Positive Role Model:** Challenge stereotypes and promote inclusivity in your own words and actions.

Conclusion:

As we journey through the teenage years with our children, we are reminded of the profound impact of mindful parenting on their emotional well-being and development. Through our nurturing presence and supportive guidance, we empower them to navigate the challenges of adolescence with courage and resilience. Let us embrace the joys and complexities of the teenage years, celebrating the milestones and cherishing the moments of connection and growth. With love, patience, and mindfulness, we lay a foundation for their future happiness and success.

Part 3: Beyond Parenting

Chapter 9: Building Resilience and Emotional Intelligence for Life

10 Tips for Fostering Ongoing Communication and Connection as Children Become Adults

1. Schedule Quality Time:

In the hustle and bustle of daily life, it's easy for family members to get caught up in their own routines and responsibilities. Yet, amidst the chaos, maintaining a strong connection with adult children remains a cornerstone of healthy family dynamics. One of the most effective ways to foster this connection is by scheduling regular quality time together.

Life's demands may pull everyone in different directions, but making a conscious effort to prioritize family time is crucial. Whether it's carving out a few hours each week for a phone call, setting aside an evening each month for a family dinner, or planning an annual vacation together, these moments of togetherness serve as anchors in the ever-changing landscape of adulthood.

Regularly scheduled quality time offers an opportunity for meaningful interactions and shared experiences. It provides a platform for open communication, genuine connection, and the cultivation of lasting memories. Whether engaged in deep conversations, shared laughter, or quiet moments of reflection, these experiences help strengthen the bond between parents and their adult children.

Moreover, scheduling quality time communicates a clear message of prioritization and commitment. It shows that despite the busyness of life, family remains a priority worth investing time and effort into. This intentional allocation of time fosters a sense of belonging, security, and closeness within the family unit.

When planning these interactions, flexibility is key. Recognize that everyone's schedules may vary, and finding a time that works for everyone may require some coordination. However, the effort invested in scheduling and prioritizing these moments of connection is well worth it in the long run.

Ultimately, scheduling quality time with adult children is not just about the quantity of time spent together but also about the quality of the interactions shared. Whether it's a simple phone call, a cozy dinner at home, or an adventurous trip abroad, these moments of togetherness contribute to the nurturing of a strong and enduring bond between parents and their adult children.

2. Active Listening:

Active listening is a cornerstone of effective communication, particularly when it comes to nurturing strong and meaningful connections with adult children. When engaging in conversations with your grown-up kids, practicing active listening demonstrates respect, empathy, and a genuine interest in their thoughts and feelings.

When your adult child is speaking, make a conscious effort to give them your undivided attention. Put away distractions such as phones, laptops, or other devices, and focus solely on what they are saying. Maintain eye contact and use nonverbal cues, such as nodding or smiling, to show that you are fully present and engaged in the conversation.

Resist the urge to interrupt or interject while your adult child is speaking. Instead, allow them to express themselves fully without interruption. This demonstrates respect for their perspective and encourages them to continue sharing their thoughts and feelings openly.

Acknowledge and validate your adult child's thoughts, feelings, and experiences. Even if you don't necessarily agree with their perspective, it's essential to show empathy and understanding. Reflect back what you hear them saying and validate their emotions by expressing empathy and compassion.

Engage in reflective listening by paraphrasing or summarizing what your adult child has said to ensure that you understand their message accurately. This not only demonstrates that you are actively listening but also helps clarify any misunderstandings and encourages further dialogue.

Encourage your adult child to expand on their thoughts and feelings by asking open-ended questions. Avoid questions that can be answered with a simple "yes" or "no" and instead, ask questions that invite deeper reflection and exploration.

Show empathy and support for your adult child's experiences, even if you haven't personally experienced the same situation. Offer words of encouragement, validation, and reassurance to let them know that you are there for them no matter what.

By practicing active listening, you create a safe and supportive environment where your adult child feels heard, understood, and valued. This lays the foundation for open and honest communication, deepening your connection and strengthening your relationship over time.

3. Respectful Communication:

Maintaining respectful communication is vital for fostering ongoing connection and understanding with adult children. Regardless of differences in opinions or perspectives, it's essential to approach conversations with openness, empathy, and a genuine desire to understand one another.

When engaging in dialogue with your adult children, prioritize mutual respect and dignity. Avoid resorting to judgmental or critical language, as this can create barriers to effective communication and strain the relationship. Instead, strive to communicate with kindness, compassion, and empathy, even when discussing challenging topics.

Acknowledge and validate your adult child's feelings and opinions, even if they differ from your own. Practice active listening by fully engaging in the conversation, refraining from interrupting, and seeking to understand their perspective without immediately jumping to conclusions or offering unsolicited advice.

Be mindful of your tone and body language during conversations with your adult children. Nonverbal cues such as facial expressions, gestures, and posture can convey messages of acceptance, understanding, or defensiveness. Aim to maintain an open and approachable demeanor that encourages your adult children to express themselves freely and honestly.

In moments of disagreement or conflict, prioritize understanding over winning the argument. Avoid escalating conflicts by remaining calm, composed, and respectful, even when emotions run high. Focus on finding common ground, exploring areas of compromise, and working together to find mutually beneficial solutions.

Strive to create a safe and nonjudgmental space where your adult children feel comfortable expressing their thoughts, feelings, and concerns openly. Be receptive to their feedback, even if it's difficult to hear, and demonstrate a willingness to learn and grow from the experience.

Ultimately, respectful communication lays the groundwork for building trust, fostering understanding, and strengthening the bond between you and your adult children. By approaching conversations with kindness, empathy, and an unwavering commitment to mutual respect, you can cultivate a relationship built on love, acceptance, and meaningful connection.

4. Acceptance and Support:

Offering acceptance and support is crucial for maintaining a strong and nurturing relationship with adult children as they navigate the complexities of adulthood. It's important to understand that acceptance doesn't equate to blind agreement or approval of every decision they make. Instead, it signifies a commitment to being there for them unconditionally, regardless of the challenges or triumphs they may encounter.

As parents, it's natural to want what's best for our children and to offer guidance and advice based on our own experiences. However, it's essential to strike a balance between providing support and allowing adult children the space to make their own decisions and learn from their experiences.

Demonstrate your unconditional love and support by being a consistent presence in their lives, both during times of joy and during periods of struggle. Let them know that you're there to offer a listening ear, a shoulder to lean on, and practical assistance whenever they need it.

Avoid imposing your own expectations or agendas onto your adult children's lives. Instead, strive to be a source of encouragement, validation, and empowerment as they navigate their unique paths.

Offer guidance and advice when requested, but respect their autonomy and decisions, even if they differ from your own.

Celebrate their achievements, no matter how big or small, and express genuine pride in their accomplishments. Acknowledge their efforts and hard work, and let them know that you believe in their abilities and potential.

During challenging times, provide a compassionate and nonjudgmental space for your adult children to express their feelings and emotions. Validate their experiences, offer empathy and understanding, and reassure them that it's okay to struggle and ask for help when needed.

Above all, cultivate a relationship based on mutual respect, trust, and unconditional love. By offering acceptance and support without conditions or expectations, you can strengthen the bond with your adult children and create a lasting foundation of love, trust, and connection.

5. Let Go of Expectations:

Letting go of expectations is a vital aspect of fostering ongoing communication and connection with adult children. As they transition into adulthood, it's essential to recognize that they are individuals with their own unique paths, dreams, and aspirations.

Releasing the expectations you held for their childhood allows you to embrace their evolving identity and needs as adults. It's natural to have hopes and dreams for your children, but clinging to rigid expectations can strain the relationship and hinder their growth and autonomy.

Instead, focus on accepting and supporting them for who they are now, rather than who you envisioned them to be. This involves letting go of preconceived notions about their career choices, relationships, or life decisions and allowing them the freedom to explore and pursue their passions.

Adjusting to their evolving needs means being flexible and adaptable in your approach to parenting. Recognize that your role may shift from being a primary caregiver to becoming a trusted advisor and confidant.

Listen attentively to their thoughts, feelings, and aspirations, and offer guidance and support when needed, but refrain from imposing your own agenda or expectations onto their lives.

Embrace their individuality and celebrate their achievements, no matter how different they may be from your own vision. By letting go of expectations and embracing their journey, you can foster a deeper sense of understanding, acceptance, and connection with your adult children.

6. Celebrate Their Achievements:

Celebrating your adult children's achievements is a powerful way to foster ongoing communication and connection. As they navigate the complexities of adulthood, it's essential to acknowledge and honor their successes, no matter how big or small.

Expressing genuine pride and joy in their accomplishments validates their efforts and strengthens your bond. Whether it's landing a new job, completing a project, or reaching a personal milestone, taking the time to celebrate their achievements shows that you are their biggest cheerleader.

Celebrate their successes with enthusiasm and sincerity, expressing admiration for their hard work and dedication. Share in their excitement and joy, and let them know how proud you are of their accomplishments.

Celebrating their achievements not only boosts their confidence and self-esteem but also reinforces your support and encouragement as a parent. It demonstrates that you are invested in their happiness and success, and that you are there to celebrate their victories every step of the way.

Take the time to acknowledge their efforts and contributions, and celebrate their achievements in meaningful ways. Whether it's hosting a small gathering, sending a heartfelt congratulatory message, or simply sharing a moment of joy together, celebrating their successes strengthens your connection and fosters a sense of mutual appreciation and respect.

7. Honoring Boundaries:

Honoring boundaries is crucial for fostering ongoing communication and connection with adult children. As they transition into adulthood, they assert their independence and autonomy more strongly, and respecting their boundaries becomes paramount in maintaining a healthy relationship.

Respecting their evolving independence means acknowledging their right to make their own decisions, even if those decisions differ from what you might have chosen for them. It involves refraining from imposing your opinions or expectations on them and allowing them the space to explore their own paths and identities.

While it's natural to want to offer support and guidance, it's essential to do so without being intrusive or overbearing. Recognize that they are capable adults capable of managing their own lives and making their own choices, even if they make mistakes along the way.

Avoiding overstepping boundaries means being mindful of their need for autonomy and privacy. Refrain from prying into their personal affairs or offering unsolicited advice unless they explicitly ask for it. Respect their decisions, even if you don't agree with them, and refrain from imposing your own agenda onto their lives.

Instead, strive to be a source of support and guidance in a way that honors their autonomy and independence. Offer assistance when needed, but let them take the lead in navigating their own challenges and decisions. Be there to listen and offer encouragement, but respect their right to make their own choices, even if they differ from what you would have chosen for them.

By honoring their boundaries, you show that you respect and value them as individuals, fostering a sense of trust and mutual respect in your relationship. This creates a foundation for open communication and connection, allowing your adult children to feel safe and supported in their interactions with you.

8. Embrace New Interests:

Embracing your adult children's new interests is an essential aspect of nurturing ongoing communication and connection with them. As they grow and develop, they may develop new hobbies, pursue different career paths, or discover new passions. Taking a genuine interest in these aspects of their lives not only demonstrates your care and support but also fosters a deeper sense of connection between you.

Showing interest in their hobbies involves more than just asking superficial questions; it requires genuine curiosity and engagement. Take the time to learn about their hobbies or interests, whether it's by attending their sports games, art exhibitions, or music performances, or simply by asking them to share their experiences and insights with you.

Show enthusiasm for their achievements and milestones, no matter how big or small, and celebrate their successes with genuine joy and pride.

Similarly, taking an interest in their careers shows that you value their professional aspirations and accomplishments. Ask them about their work, their goals, and their challenges, and offer support and encouragement as they navigate their career paths. Offer words of encouragement and advice when needed, but also respect their autonomy and decisions in their professional lives.

Finally, showing interest in their passions involves supporting their personal growth and self-discovery. Whether they're pursuing a new hobby, embarking on a creative project, or exploring a new area of interest, be there to cheer them on and offer encouragement along the way. Share in their excitement and enthusiasm, and let them know that you're proud of their efforts and achievements.

By embracing your adult children's new interests, you demonstrate your love, support, and genuine care for them as individuals. This fosters a deeper connection between you and strengthens your relationship, allowing you to share in each other's joys, challenges, and experiences as they continue to grow and evolve.

9. Embrace New Roles:

As your children transition into adulthood and potentially become parents themselves, your role in their lives evolves in significant ways. Embracing these new roles with sensitivity and respect is crucial for fostering ongoing communication and connection with them.

One of the most significant new roles you may take on is that of a grandparent. Becoming a grandparent is a unique and rewarding experience that brings its own set of joys and challenges. As a grandparent, you have the opportunity to offer love, support, and guidance to your grandchildren while respecting the boundaries and parenting choices of their parents.

Celebrate the joy of grandparenthood by cherishing the special moments you share with your grandchildren. Whether it's cuddling a newborn baby, reading stories to a toddler, or playing games with older grandchildren, savor these precious moments and create lasting memories together.

At the same time, it's essential to recognize and respect the authority of your adult children as parents. While you may have valuable wisdom and experience to offer, avoid overstepping boundaries or imposing your own parenting style on your children. Instead, offer support and guidance when asked, and be willing to step back and let your children take the lead in parenting their own children.

Maintaining open communication with your adult children about their parenting preferences, concerns, and needs is key to navigating this new role successfully. Listen attentively to their thoughts and feelings, and offer your support and encouragement as they navigate the joys and challenges of parenthood.

By embracing your new roles as your children become parents themselves, you can foster a deeper connection with them and build a strong foundation for your relationship to continue to grow and evolve in the years to come. Celebrate the joys of grandparenthood while respecting the autonomy and choices of your adult children, and cherish the unique bond that family brings.

10. Maintain Shared Traditions and Focus on Shared Values:

Maintaining shared traditions and focusing on shared values are powerful ways to foster ongoing communication and connection with adult children. These traditions serve as anchors that ground your family in a sense of belonging and continuity, regardless of the changes and transitions that come with adulthood.

Whether it's celebrating holidays, birthdays, or other special occasions, these shared traditions provide opportunities for family members to come together, reminisce about past experiences, and create new memories. They offer a sense of stability and connection, reinforcing the bonds that tie your family together.

In addition to maintaining existing traditions, consider creating new ones that are meaningful and relevant to your family's evolving dynamics. This could involve starting new rituals or activities that reflect the interests and values of your adult children. For example, you might establish a monthly family game night, organize an annual family vacation, or participate in volunteer activities together.

The key is to involve your adult children in the process of creating and upholding these traditions, ensuring that they feel a sense of ownership and investment in preserving family rituals. This collaborative approach strengthens the sense of unity and togetherness within the family and fosters a deeper connection between generations.

Furthermore, focusing on shared values provides a guiding framework for your family's interactions and decisions. By identifying and affirming the values that are important to your family—such as honesty, respect, compassion, and resilience—you create a common language and set of principles that guide your relationships with one another.

Encourage open discussions about these values and how they manifest in your family's daily life. Share stories and anecdotes that illustrate these values in action, and reinforce their importance through your words and actions.

By maintaining shared traditions and focusing on shared values, you create opportunities for meaningful connection and communication with your adult children. These rituals and principles serve as touchstones that strengthen the bonds of family and create a sense of belonging that endures across generations.

.

Chapter 10: Resources and Conclusion

Resources for Mindful Parenting

In your journey of mindful parenting, having access to resources can be invaluable in supporting your efforts to nurture emotional intelligence and strengthen the parent-child bond. Here are some resources to explore:

Books:

1. "Parenting from the Inside Out: How a Deeper Self-Understanding Can Help You Raise Children Who Thrive" by Mary Hartzell, MEd & Daniel J. Siegel, MD

2. "Everyday Blessings: The Inner Work of Mindful Parenting" by Myla & Jon Kabat-Zinn

3. "Mindful Parenting: A Guide for Mental Health Practitioners" by Susan Bogels & Kathleen Restifo

4. "The Complete Buddhism for Mothers" by Sarah Napthali

5. "Buddha Mom: A Journey Through Mindful Mothering" by Jacqueline Kramer

6. "Wherever You Go, There You Are" by Jon Kabat-Zinn, MD

7. "Mindfulness in Plain English" by Bhante Gunaratana, PhD (Henepola Gunaratana)

8. "The Whole-Brain Child" by Daniel J. Siegel and Tina Payne Bryson.

9. "Peaceful Parent, Happy Kids" by Dr. Laura Markham.

10. "Parenting from the Inside Out" by Daniel J. Siegel and Mary Hartzell.

Websites:

1. Insight Meditation of Cleveland: imcleveland.org

2. Mindful Parenting: mindfulparenting.com

3. Child Mind Institute: childmind.org

4. Mindful Mama Mentor: mindfulmamamentor.com

Organizations:

1. Stanford University's Division of Child and Adolescent Psychiatry and Child Development: **https://med.stanford.edu/ childpsychiatry/parenting/topics/mindfulparenting.html**

2. Happily Family: **https://happilyfamily.com**

Online Courses and Workshops:

1. Mindful Schools (**https://www.mindfulschools.org**/): Mindful Schools offers online courses and workshops designed to teach mindfulness skills to parents and educators.

2. The Gottman Institute (**https://www.gottman.com**/): The Gottman Institute provides resources and workshops focused on strengthening parent-child relationships through research-based techniques.

3. Positive Discipline Association (**https://www.positivediscipline.org**/): The Positive Discipline Association offers online workshops and resources for parents seeking positive discipline strategies.

Mindfulness Apps:

1. Headspace: The Headspace app offers guided meditations, mindfulness exercises, and sleep sounds that can be helpful for both parents and children.

2. Calm: Calm provides meditation sessions, sleep stories, and relaxation techniques to help reduce stress and promote emotional well-being.

3. Insight Timer: Insight Timer offers a vast library of guided meditations, music tracks, and talks on mindfulness and self-care.

These resources cover a range of perspectives and approaches to mindful parenting, including practical guides, personal reflections, and educational programs. They offer insights into mindfulness practices, communication strategies, and techniques for managing stress and emotions in parenting.

Conclusion:

The Mindful Parenting Journey Continues:

"The Mindful Parenting Journey Continues" is the culmination of a transformative exploration into the art of mindful parenting, encapsulating the essence of fostering emotional intelligence, strengthening parent-child connections, and nurturing resilient, well-adjusted children. Throughout this journey, we have delved into the depths of self-awareness, empathy, and conscious communication, discovering the profound impact of mindfulness on our parenting approach.

At the heart of this book lies the core message that mindful parenting is not a destination but a continuous journey—a journey of growth, learning, and evolution. It is a journey that begins with the recognition that parenting is as much about our own inner journey as it is about guiding our children. By cultivating mindfulness in our daily lives, we embark on a path of self-discovery, gaining deeper insights into our thoughts, emotions, and reactions.

As we reflect on the lessons learned and the practices embraced, we are reminded of the power of presence—the simple act of being fully engaged and attuned to our children's needs, emotions, and experiences. Mindful parenting invites us to meet each moment with intentionality and compassion, fostering a nurturing environment where our children can thrive.

As parents, we encounter myriad challenges and triumphs, joys and struggles, but through it all, we remain steadfast in our commitment to mindful parenting. We recognize that there will be moments of doubt, frustration, and uncertainty, but we approach them with kindness, patience, and resilience.

In the pages of this book, we have explored practical strategies, insightful reflections, and inspiring stories that illuminate the path of mindful parenting. As we continue our journey, let us carry with us the wisdom gained, the lessons learned, and the connections forged.

My Last Words to Parents

To all the parents embarking on this lifelong journey, I offer words of encouragement and inspiration. Trust in your innate wisdom and intuition as a parent. Embrace each moment as an opportunity for growth and learning. And above all, cultivate love, acceptance, and presence in your relationships with your children. May your journey of mindful parenting be filled with grace, authenticity, and profound connection, enriching the lives of both you and your children for years to come.

About the Author

Neo K. Bika is a woman of faith, family, and fostering emotional intelligence in children and as a pastor's wife, she understands the importance of strong values and building a supportive community. As a mother of three and a sibling of seven, she's well-versed in the joys and challenges of raising a vibrant household. For nearly two decades, Neo has poured her passion into children's ministry, guiding young minds and hearts. This experience, coupled with her own journey in motherhood, fueled her to write this book.